WINNING WITH STYLE

SIX PROVEN STRATEGIES TO FORGE POWERFUL RELATIONSHIPS

Dr. John W. Hanes

Winning with Style:
Six Proven Strategies to Forge Powerful Relationships
By Dr. John W. Hanes
1. BUS071000 BUSINESS & ECONOMICS / Leadership
2. EDU032000 EDUCATION / Leadership
3. BUS041000 BUSINESS & ECONOMICS / Management

ISBN Hardcover: 978-1-935953-82-1

Printed in the United States of America
Authority Publishing
11230 Gold Express Dr. #310-413
Gold River, CA 95670
800-877-1097
www.AuthorityPublishing.com

CONTENTS

To My Wife, Mariann

A Master Relationship Builder
And the Most Wonderful Woman
I Have Ever Known

ACKNOWLEDGEMENTS

THIS BOOK IS a collaborative effort and is the result of the contribution of a great many people:

My Family: Mariann, Chad, Marinda, Ryan, Dwight, and Leslie, whom I love deeply. They bring considerable joy and help me keep the challenges in life in proper perspective.

My Parents: Jack and Betty grounded me with solid values, taught me the proper way to treat people, and sacrificed mightily so that I had the opportunity to get a college education.

My Granddaughter: Maddie, you are only three months old as of this writing, but you have made me aware of the beauty and innocence of life.

My Mentors and Teachers: Jim Wright, John Kindler, Tom Downham, Jerry Edge, and Dr. John Hanson, who showed me the ropes of the business world. Dr. Joe Rost, Dr. Don Penner, and Dr. Bill Hitt, who were the greatest of teachers.

My Assistant: Ronelle Melton, who diligently typed my manuscript and provided encouragement that my book had something important to say.

My Editors: Paul Zieke and Mark Meyer, whose trained eyes and attention to detail helped me avoid critical errors and omissions.

My Project Manager: Stephanie Chandler at Authority Publishing. Once again, you proved to be a wizard and true professional.

Your coordination skills and depth of knowledge of the publishing world is truly amazing.

My Clients: Over the past 31 years, they have taught me far more than I have ever taught them.

My world-class leaders and friends who agreed to be interviewed for this book: Each of you brought the strategies in the book to life.

- Launie Fleming, Group CEO, Senior Aerospace Corporation
- Major General Steve Sargeant (Ret.), CEO, Marvin Test Solutions
- Fred Howard, Former CEO, Metagenics and Serial Entrepreneur
- Bob Dobbs, Vice President, Great American Financial
- Chris Carroll, Senior Vice President, Callaway Golf
- Karen Bomba, CEO, Morpho Detection
- Ben Diachun, CEO, Scaled Composites
- Doug Shane, CEO, The Spaceship Company
- Kim Chiodi, Senior Vice President, Western Southern Financial Group
- Shawn Imitates-Dog, Vice President, Live Nation
- John Rae, Vice President, Cleveland/Srixon Golf
- Michelle Vargas, Director, NFP
- Teresa Schlegel, Vice President, Packsize
- Hedley Lawson, CEO, Aligned Growth Partners
- Dr. Mike Burns, CEO, Ferndale Pharma Group
- Brian Burke, President, Calgary Flames
- Mark Murphy, President and CEO, Green Bay Packers
- Dr. Peter B. Angood, CEO, American Association for Physician Leadership

Despite all this help, I am sure that I failed to cite someone or some work along the way that contributed something of value to this book. For these, I ask your forgiveness and accept full responsibility.

INTRODUCTION

THIS IS A book about the process of building powerful relationships. Interacting with one another, as bosses leading associates, peers influencing peers, salespeople attempting to win customer business, or wives dealing with their husbands, the inescapable truth is that our success or failure is a direct result of our ability to create and sustain productive, reciprocal relationships.

From getting the best deal on buying things to asking your employer for a pay raise, from negotiating with suppliers to resolving conflicts within a team, in any situation where two or more people have competing needs or desires, developing mutually satisfying relationships is an essential part of getting what you want out of life.

Too many leaders pay little or no attention to the relational aspects of business. They share the fantasy that with just developing the right strategy, having the lowest price or the best quality, and exerting greater effort, they can accomplish anything – that their "style" does not really matter. Yet my 41-year career working with leaders from over 1,700 organizations has provided me with clear and compelling evidence that this simply is not the case. Most leaders who fail to live up to their potential crash and burn because of their inability or unwillingness to relate well with key people they encounter. Most do not discover this essential truth until it is too late, and some never get it at all. Others do understand the importance of creating positive relationships but are ill equipped for building them due to a lack of knowledge or poor skill in putting into practice what they do know.

We find ourselves in an era where the "new normal" is one of polarized conflict. In politics, in the media, and even in our social circles, everyone seems to be righteously indignant, with few even willing to consider the views of someone else. Rather than seeking to understand another's philosophy or idea, we cling to deeply entrenched positions, aggressively pursuing our agendas or turning a blind eye to others' needs. We become governed more by our emotions than by carefully crafted discourse.

We also work in a world where hierarchy is on its way out and a more democratic way of leading is called for. Though they differ in more ways than they are similar, Generation X associates and Millennials each reject out of hand the old command and control style of leadership. Leading in a more networked and collaborative manner has proven to be one of the most challenging tasks facing virtually every leader I encounter these days in both sports and business.

Take pro football, for instance. In the old days (not that long ago), coaches decided, players executed, and that was the end of it. In one of many examples I could share, on December 30, 2015, Philadelphia Eagles Owner Jeffrey Lurie unceremoniously dismissed Chip Kelly as head coach. Lurie reportedly said, "Our next coach needs to be able to open his heart to everyone in the organization if he wants to achieve maximum success. Relationships and communication needs to improve with everyone in the Eagles organization." This statement was a clear signal that it was not wins and losses that caused Kelly's demise (he had won 27 games in 3 seasons) – it was his failure to effectively engage with others. Not coincidentally, few Eagles players seemed upset at his departure.[1] Amazingly, the San Francisco 49ers immediately hired Kelly as their new head coach, evidently rejecting the view that past behavior is the best indicator of future behavior. His behavior predictably did not change, and he was summarily fired after one season, posting a dismal 2-14 record. Few 49er players had anything positive to say about their deposed coach.

Effective relationship building is about extensive observation, advance preparation, authentic communication, and a sincere desire to not just meet your own needs, but those of others with whom you interact. Great relationships have three elements:

1. They begin with a deep and honest understanding of yourself, something that many people find difficult to do or accept.
2. Next comes attempting to learn as much as you can about the style and desires of the people you will be interacting with – perhaps even more fully than they understand themselves.
3. Finally, it is about learning to influence others by creating a mutually satisfying proposition based upon data, heartfelt emotion, ego gratification, or shared bottom-line goals.

Perhaps no greater testimonial to this process has come from that of the University of Alabama football program. Its leader, Head Coach Nick Saban, is as tough and no-nonsense as they come. Yet he gives partial credit for the team's unparalleled success (four NCAA Division I Championships under Saban) to a focus on interpersonal style, team dynamics, effective communication, and relationship building. In the words of Coach Saban, "It gave us the information about our players and insight about my coaches that let everyone know how others think and how they work. It helps us manage, work with, and motivate others better because we now realize everyone has a different style."[2]

These days, most organizations in both business and sports are comprised of members with diverse skills, backgrounds, and personalities – differences in gender, race, age, ethnicity, sexual preferences, and religion create a wealth of talent and perspective that the organization can capitalize upon. However, the art of successfully leading these diverse individuals presents a much more complex challenge than when everyone is mostly the same.

Winning with Style introduces Six Leadership Strategies and numerous tactics which will allow you to recognize, understand, relate to, and influence different types of people. You will learn to minimize conflict and get greater results from both people similar in "style" to you, as well as those whose "style" is different. You will gain insight into how to deliver more effective business or sales presentations and understand the keys to unlocking the spirit and commitment of all members of your team. You will hear real-world stories from dozens of successful leaders, often in their own words, to make the concepts come alive.

There are no quick fixes or "silver bullets" for relating well to others. Relationships are complicated and often messy. But by putting in the effort to understand and apply the principles and behaviors outlined in this book, you can greatly increase your odds of success. You will find the six strategies to be self-evident, meaning they make so much sense it will be hard to mount an argument against them. That does not mean you will be an overnight sensation in implementing them. But with a little practice, they will become second nature.

Most of my advice in this book is timeless. Yes, the world continues to change and Boomers are different than Gen Xers, and they in turn are not like the Millennials, but the fundamental prescriptions have not changed much since I began my career because deep down people are driven by many of the same needs and desires as people were a millennium ago. The way we must deal with these needs and desires if we want to be successful has to change, but the basic needs we all try to satisfy remain the same.

Of course, no guide on interpersonal effectiveness can cover every situation you encounter. Further, not every relationship can be salvaged, nor is it advisable that every relationship should be saved. Perhaps there is so much prior "bad blood" that the ability to resuscitate it is impossible. But one of the strengths of *Winning with Style* is that it offers insights and suggestions on a wide-ranging number of factors that have been "battle tested" by the over 27,000 managers who have attended my Dr. John W. Hanes Leadership Academy Seminars. Nine out of ten leaders who went through the workshop and later applied the lessons said they achieved happier, less stressful, and more productive relationships with people both at home and at work. The book is laid out as follows:

Chapter 1: Allows you to assess your basic Interpersonal Style

Chapter 2: Gives advice on how to win with the strengths of your style

Chapter 3: Outlines the eight core competencies of highly influential people

Chapter 4: Shows you ways to build a power base

Chapter 5: Tells you how to create trust, which cements relationships

Chapter 6: Helps you avoid the Seven Deadly Relationship Sins

Chapter 7: Provides prescriptions on how to act professionally at work

It is my hope that the ideas contained in this book will cause you to see options and avenues of dealing effectively with others that might not have been visible to you before. Let the journey begin!

CHAPTER 1

WHAT IS YOUR INTERPERSONAL STYLE?

Interpersonal Preferences Profile

THIS PROFILE WAS created to help you assess the manner in which you prefer to act with other people. Be consistent throughout the profile in thinking about work situations as opposed to home situations.

To get the most accurate results, put yourself in a relaxed frame of mind and work quickly – do not overthink your responses.

Each item contains three different word or behavioral choices. You are to distribute 5 points among the three choices to indicate how characteristic each behavior is of you. You can distribute the 5 points in any combination you choose; including allocating zero points for a behavior, but always use all 5 points and never more than 5 points for each of the 40 sets of choices.

Example

Results Oriented 2		Factual 2		Supportive 1	
1	Leading	___	Independently contributing	___	Supporting	___
2	Tenacious	___	Studious and Careful	___	A team player	___
3	Enjoy selling	___	Enjoy research	___	Enjoy socializing	___
4	Fast to seize opportunities	___	Wary of acting too quickly	___	Quick to meet others' needs	___
5	Seek to be quickly respected by others	___	Cautious at first around others	___	Seek to be quickly liked by others	___
6	Concerned with influencing others	___	Concerned with details	___	Concerned with finding a win-win	___
7	Like to be called upon to give direction	___	Like to self-supervise	___	Like to contribute to the greater good	___
8	Make tough decisions quickly	___	Do extensive research before deciding	___	Assist others in deciding	___
9	An ambitious self-starter	___	Unbending in my principals	___	Loyal to my friends	___
10	Proactive	___	Practical and organized	___	Responsive to others	___
11	Seen as being a winner	___	Respected for being fair	___	Appreciated for being helpful	___
12	Productive	___	Intelligent and well-read	___	Care about other people's needs	___
13	Dislike being taken advantage of	___	Dislike being seen as impulsive	___	Dislike confrontations with others	___
14	Visionary	___	Systematic	___	Meet others' needs	___
15	Push back when I disagree	___	Hold my ground but seek more info	___	Give in quicker than I should	___
16	Sell or Decide	___	Design or Build	___	Teach or Coach	___
17	Persuasive but a little pushy	___	Objective and Controlled	___	Open and Likeable	___

18	Compete to win	___	Avoid open confrontation	___	Accommodate to preserve Relationships	___
19	Excited by risk	___	Avoid or minimize risk	___	Take some risks	___
20	Influence with conviction	___	Appeal to logic	___	Concentrate on building the relationship	___
21	Ambitious	___	Analytical	___	Appreciative	___
22	Competitive	___	Comprehensive	___	Approachable	___
23	Strong conviction	___	Conscientious	___	Considerate	___
24	Decisive	___	Conservative	___	Cooperative	___
25	Demanding	___	Consistent	___	Dependable	___
26	Efficient	___	Detail Oriented	___	Empathetic	___
27	Energetic	___	Ethical	___	Encouraging	___
28	Fast-Paced	___	Logical	___	Easy to read	___
29	Forceful	___	Methodical	___	Friendly	___
30	Influential	___	Orderly	___	Good Listener	___
31	Initiating	___	Predictable	___	Idealistic	___
32	Opinionated	___	Principled	___	Loyal	___
33	Persevering	___	Rational	___	Open	___
34	Persistent	___	Reserved	___	Patient	___
35	Persuasive	___	Intellectual	___	People Oriented	___
36	Politically Savvy	___	Independent	___	Service Oriented	___
37	Results Oriented	___	Factual	___	Supportive	___
38	Self-Confident	___	Thorough	___	Tactful	___
39	Self-Starter	___	Trusted	___	Team Player	___
40	Sense of Urgency	___	Uncompromising	___	Understanding	___

Total Column A ___ **Total Column B** ___ **Total Column C** ___

3

Scoring Instructions

Add up the numbers in the three columns (A, B, and C). The total should equal 200.

If Column A is the highest of the three and it is more than 4 points higher than the next highest column, you prefer the Ruby Style.

If Column B is highest of the three and it is more than 4 points higher than the next highest column, you prefer the Emerald Style.

If Column C is the highest of the three and it is more than 4 points higher than the next highest column, you prefer the Sapphire Style.

If Columns A and B are within 4 points of one another, and are more than 4 points higher than Column C, you prefer the Topaz Style.

If Columns A and C are within 4 points of one another and are more than 4 points higher than Column B, then you prefer the Fire Opal Style.

If Columns B and C are within 4 points of one another and are more than 4 points higher than Column A, then you prefer the Aquamarine Style.

If all three columns are within 4 points of one another, you are about 1 in 200 people. You do not exhibit a clear preference and are multi-faceted. The good news is that you probably get along well with most people. Potentially bad news is that you may be difficult for others to understand because your preferences are not as obvious as the other six styles.

My Style Is _____

CHAPTER 2

STRATEGY 1 – WIN WITH THE STRENGTH OF YOUR STYLE

"Having close, satisfying relationships is the only way
to make it through life without going crazy."

Dennis Prager

IT IS WIDELY accepted in mainstream behavioral psychology that certain behavioral traits tend to cluster together to form personality "styles". The debate among psychologists and researchers centers around two questions:

1. What are the most important underlying motives or preferences that form these "styles"?
2. How many different "styles" result from the various combinations of these underlying motives or preferences?

My 41 years of dealing with leaders has repeatedly shown me that all human beings seem to possess some amount of three critically important preferences. These foundational preferences are:

1. The importance one places on control, achievement and the desire to take risks (what I call a Ruby).

2. The desire for data, structure, and conservatism in risk taking (what I call Emerald).

3. The desire for positive relationships, social interaction, and the support of others (what I call Sapphire).

These foundational preferences cause us to gravitate towards doing things in a certain way. It is kind of like being predisposed to predominately using your left hand or your right hand. Most people have a preference for using one hand over the other. Of course, we use both hands throughout each day, and we can easily switch hands, but we instinctively have a preference for one hand over the other. Our foundational behavioral preferences function in much the same way.

In my model, we look at six interpersonal styles. Three styles are the ones described above – Ruby, Emerald and Sapphire. These are the "core" styles. The three additional styles are blends of two of the three core preferences. The Fire Opal Style is a strong blend of control and achievement with the desire for positive supportive relationships with others. The Aquamarine Style is a strong combination of the need for structure and data with the desire to build positive relationships and support others. The Topaz Style has a dual focus on control and achievement with a high need for data and structure.

I use gemstones as a way to describe the six styles. Each of these gemstones is unique. No gemstone is inherently more valuable than another; just as no one style is inherently more desirable than another. Each style has typical potential strengths that a person can draw upon in interactions with others. And, each style has common potential pitfalls that can cause problems for a person in his/her dealings with others.

By the time one is 16 years old, our *basic* style preferences are pretty much locked in. Sure, they can be modified to a degree, which is what I hope you will choose to do after reading this book. But, it is unlikely that a person who has a strong preference will change that preference in a dramatic way unless certain potentially life-changing events were to occur. The most prominent examples of dramatic shifts typically happen upon the death of a child, a personal near-death experience, an unexpected divorce, or the loss of a job that a person really loves.

The good news is that to become interpersonally adept, one does not have to change dramatically. One needs to simply adjust temporarily to the demands of the situation by dredging up the helpful parts of our weaker preferences. This is something we are all capable of doing – some more easily than others. And, since we all have some of each of the core preferences within us, these adjustments will not seem phony or insincere as they are also elements of who we are as complex people.

It is kind of like a resume. Your resume should always be 100% truthful. However, if you are applying for a job as an engineer, your resume should showcase your *engineering* qualifications. If instead, you are applying for an *engineering management* position, your resume should emphasize your *management* skills. You are still the same person, just putting a different "face on" based upon the requirements of the position.

Tales from the Workplace

Bill Gross, co-founder of PIMCO, one of the largest investment firms in the world, reportedly chased away his hand-picked successor, Mohamed El-Erian, because of his temper and "intense interpersonal style." According to a story in the *Wall Street Journal*, associates at PIMCO were so intimidated by their patriarch that they were afraid to speak their minds. Later, in an interview with *Bloomberg Businessweek*, Gross asked a rhetorical question, "Am I really such a jerk?" Then upon reflection, he admitted that he was, in fact, too dominant and too intimidating. The challenge, he said, was to find a way to interact in a manner that values his deputies while continuing to produce great results for his clients.[1]

This interpersonal model is simple to understand, easy to remember, and accurate in describing the *basic* personality of the majority of people you are likely to interact with at work or home. It will not tell you *in-depth* what makes a person "tick." It is merely meant to be a starting point to make sure you are in the right ballpark when it comes to relating to others. Therefore, you should avoid the temptation to place people in rigid boxes or expect that every aspect of their behavior can be explained by these six "styles." After all, there are billions of people in the world, and my model consists of only six styles. But, because it concentrates on patterns of behavior that people exhibit to the outer world, it can give us valuable insight into what is going on inside that person's head. With a little practice, you will instantly be able to see the differences in these patterns and adjust accordingly the way you approach people who seem to exhibit these six styles.

Let's begin by describing some of the fundamental characteristics of each gemstone.

The Ruby Style

The most powerful traits of strong Ruby personalities are their preference for control, bottom-line achievement, and taking risks. They are fast-paced, opinionated, and often try and dominate others in business meetings. Others usually see them as competitive, decisive, forceful, self-confident, impatient, and goal oriented. The Ruby type tackles conflict, change, and difficult decisions head on. They tend to be comfortable with ambiguity and dislike onerous policies, procedures, and rules. They look for the most time-efficient way to accomplish their goals. Ruby types hate to be micromanaged, bore quickly, look to make immediate impact, and are action oriented.

The Ruby type can be easily motivated by external factors such as pay, special perks, trophies, plaques, certificates, titles, being given more formal authority, and anything that strokes their ego. They become focused under intense time pressure and are classic multitaskers. They perform particularly well in crises situations.

On the downside, the Ruby type is often seen as abrasive, blunt, pushy, impatient, self-centered, and overly critical of others. They have a tendency to try and circumvent the rules when it is to their advantage to do so. They can be autocratic or dictatorial at times and do not handle criticism well.

The Ruby personality type gravitates to careers such as high-level corporate executives, small-business owners, non-technical sales, and military officers. In the general population, about 20 percent of people exhibit the Ruby style, but in management positions, that percentage doubles to 40 percent.

A Quick Guide to the Ruby Style

Positive Traits	Negative Traits
Efficient	Abrasive
Decisive	Blunt
Self-Starter	Autocratic
Results Oriented	Pushy/Overbearing
Sense of Urgency	Critical
Has Conviction	Self-Centered
Likes Challenge	Flout the Rules
Handles Crises well	Impatient

Influencing Rubies

- Be quick and to the point.
- Use bullet items to make key points.
- Minimize the amount and complexity of data presented.
- Use "executive summary" format, i.e. background of the issue, the problem, two or three alternatives, and your conclusions.
- Use forcefulness in presenting – they may not take the time to understand your presentation, but they will be sold by your conviction.
- Use simple charts, graphs, and visuals. Avoid tables of black and white numbers.
- Rubies do not mind risk. In their minds, if there is no risk, there is little excitement.

- Rubies buy the benefits of things and are not impressed by features and how things work.
- Rubies rarely check references or do extensive research. They pride themselves on their decisiveness.
- Do not compete with, demean, or insult Rubies.
- Do not be put off if Rubies ask what appear to be direct or confrontational questions. That is just their way of judging your conviction.
- Do not expect or try to create warm, fuzzy feelings with Rubies. Be content with achieving the goal.
- Do not tell jokes or engage in much small talk. Rubies usually have two or three things they cannot wait to get to, so don't waste their time.

Suggestions for Rubies when Interacting with Emeralds

- State your position objectively including possible weaknesses of your argument.
- Allow Emeralds time to think. They get stressed under time pressure.
- Don't discount their ideas. Seek their rationale.
- Recognize Emeralds are proud of their research and want to show it to you.
- Try and avoid seeming impatient with their slow speed and plethora of questions.
- Be less pushy and blunt.
- Demonstrate that you understand the risks and have taken steps to mitigate or eliminate them.
- Do not speak with too much passion or emotion.

Suggestions for Rubies Interacting with Sapphires

- Involve Sapphires as partners.
- Actively listen and do not cut them off.
- Be very sensitive in criticizing them. Start with a positive and end with a positive.

- Ask them how they would do things. When you ask questions, let them know why you are asking them.
- In meetings, try and get Sapphires to speak before stating your position.
- Build a relationship by getting to know them and allowing them to get comfortable with you.

Famous People who exhibit the Ruby Style

None of the following people have been assessed on the Interpersonal Preferences Profile, but each seem to exhibit many of the characteristics associated with the Ruby Style.

- Donald Trump – President of the United States
- Richard Nixon – President of the United States
- Lyndon Johnson – President of the United States
- Anna Wintour – Editor, *Vogue Magazine*
- Ellen Kullman – CEO, DuPont
- Bill Gross – Co-Founder, PIMCO
- Charles Koch – Billionaire
- Mark Cuban – Owner, Dallas Mavericks
- Sheryl Sandberg – COO, Facebook
- Mike Shanahan – Super Bowl-winning Coach, Denver Broncos
- Bob Knight – NCAA Basketball Head Coach, National Champion, Indiana Hoosiers

Tales from the Workplace

Major General (Retired) Steve Sargeant, CEO of Marvin Test Solutions, attributes a great deal of his success as a leader to a practice of valuing people developed and implemented over his 34-year career as an active duty military officer and practiced over the past five years as a CEO. A few nuggets of wisdom from our conversation are as follows:

- When taking over a business or command from someone, express great respect to them for what they have built and sing their praises to lower-level members in the organization. Never disparage things they have done or decisions they have made, even if these decisions run counter to how you would have handled things. Having acted in this manner will allow you to use the foundation they have laid to set the bar higher without generating resistance from them or their supporters.

- Instead of trying to force your ideas or solutions to problems on your staff, try and find ways to start a dialogue on the issue. Ask a lot of questions centered on what they think the problem or solution to be. Have patience, do not try and solve the problem right there and then. Allow your prodding on the issue to percolate in their minds. Most of the time, they will come back to you wanting further discussion on the matter. It is much easier to implement change if the impetus for it comes from the people who need to take the actions necessary to cause the change to happen.

- If you are a "Ruby," at times you will have to put the brakes on your assertive personality and operate with a more observant, deliberate style. You may have to take your pride of authorship and ego and put it where it should be, in the bottom of the desk drawer, if you really want to get things done.

> - Leadership is about building a trust-based relationship with your staff, letting them know that you are not coming in with a preconceived game plan. Then learn together, grow together, jointly develop a strategy to create shared buy in, and open up participation to other key players at lower levels. Communication must be open and regular with your motives transparent throughout the organization.

The Emerald Style

The most powerful traits of Emeralds are their preference for deep analysis, structure, and minimizing risk. They approach decision-making and change cautiously. They tend to be tentative, reserved communicators. The vast majority of Emeralds are socially introverted. Emeralds speak more slowly and at a lower volume than Rubies. They seldom take the initiative in meetings or social gatherings.

Emerald types dislike ambiguity, sloppy analysis, and poorly thought-out decisions. They are analytical and systematic problem solvers. At work, they like structure, clear role definition, systems, processes, and procedures. Their strongest motivation is often to solve difficult, intractable problems that have stymied others.

Emeralds typically prefer to contribute individually, versus working in teams. When they do work with others, they prefer to do so with peers whom they respect, and they like a stability of membership within the team. They have a strong need to know how things work. Planning is their way of reducing risk and improving their odds in uncertain situations.

Emeralds make decisions based upon logic and data. At times, they may become mired in analysis. They have a difficult time making decisions under time pressure and when there are many options. More extreme Emeralds are perfectionists. In their way of thinking, people are unpredictable and emotions complicate matters.

Emeralds are often guarded about their personal lives when interacting with others and can be seen as cool, aloof, and impersonal. Most Emeralds tend to be well read and possess an above-average vocabulary, but seem to have trouble communicating to people who are less studious in their areas of expertise. They can come across as condescending and have a tendency to nitpick at things most others see as inconsequential. As you might imagine, the toughest supervisory challenge is Emeralds working for Rubies or Rubies working for Emeralds. They desperately need one another but often frustrate one another.

The Emerald Style gravitates to careers in back room support functions such as information technology, contracts, purchasing, science, engineering, the research arm of the legal department, and the compensation and benefits side of the human resources function. In the general population, Emeralds make up about 15 percent of people and comprise about 20 percent of those in management positions.

A Quick Guide to the Emerald Style

Positive Traits	Negative Traits
Comprehensive	Impersonal
Conscientious	Insensitive
Consistent	Condescending
Logical	Indecisive
Factual	Guarded
Systematic	Risk Averse
Detail Oriented	Nitpicking
Solve Complex Problems	Resist Change
Intellectually Curious	Socially Awkward

Influencing Emeralds

- Work through complex charts at a methodical pace.
- Show a logical train of thought, i.e. "A" leads to "B" which leads to "C" and causes "D."

- Present lots of data; show how it was developed and any assumptions that went into it.
- Since Emeralds hate risk, reduce it whenever possible.
- Emeralds must understand the features and how things work before they can buy any potential benefits.
- Be patient and be prepared for them to ask a lot of questions.
- Be careful making errors of fact. The Emerald will probably catch the errors and your credibility in every other area will be undermined.
- Give Emeralds a few well-researched options, as they tend to get paralyzed by too many choices.
- Don't waste time with small talk and jokes. They see this as superfluous.
- Emphasize your degrees, credentials, and track record.
- Give Emeralds a take-away piece to study. When you follow up, make it low risk for them to "buy."
- Emeralds respond to third-party testimonials from independent sources, and they like performance guarantees.
- Don't be put off if Emeralds do not give off body language, facial expressions, or voice tone that might indicate comfort with your idea or proposal. They can be very hard to read.

Suggestions for Emeralds when Interacting with Rubies

- Take a firmer position on issues – do not waffle.
- Pick up your pace a couple of notches.
- Do not get offended if Rubies do not want to see your "homework."
- See the "political" side of people as a challenge, not a turnoff.
- Cut your presentation down to the bare minimum.
- Present your ideas with passion and conviction.
- Appeal to the Ruby ego.

Suggestions For Emeralds When Interacting with Sapphires

- Build a personal relationship. If they trust you, they will trust your data, analysis, and conclusions.
- Engage in small talk before you begin presenting.
- Open up about yourself.
- Cut your presentation down to the bare minimum.
- Smile frequently, make eye contact, call them by name, dress casually, and engage them in the conversation.
- Be proactive in solving any personality conflicts that may occur.
- Try to find some common ground to talk about.
- Sapphires love sincere compliments.
- Do not make Sapphires feel intellectually insecure.

Famous People Who Exhibit the Emerald Style

None of the following people have been assessed on the Interpersonal Preferences Profile, but each seem to exhibit many of the characteristics associated with the Emerald Style.

- Jimmy Carter – President of the United States
- Janet Yellen – Chairwoman of the Federal Reserve
- Janet Reno – Former Attorney General
- Bill Belichick – Head Coach, Super Bowl Champion, New England Patriots
- Adam Silver – NBA Commissioner
- Meg Whitman – CEO, Hewlett Packard
- Irene Rosenfeld – CEO, Mondelēz International
- Mark Parker – CEO, Nike
- Jeb Bush – Former Governor, State of Florida
- Mark Zuckerberg – Founder, Facebook

Tales from the Workplace

At the ripe old age of 22, my first job out of college was as an advance scout for the defending Super Bowl Champion Pittsburgh Steelers. I was hired on a contract basis reporting directly to Head Coach Chuck Noll, who had already won two Super Bowls and would go on to win two more. A last-minute medical issue had sidelined one of the Steelers pro scouts for the season and opened the door for me to step into the role at the eleventh hour. I will always remember my interview with Coach Noll, who years later I came to find out was an extreme Emerald. My interview concluded with him saying, "You are not much kid, but you are better than us going with the job unfilled, so go down to payroll and let them know I hired you – the job starts tomorrow." Not exactly a real confidence builder.

In the NFL, coaches typically only focus one week out and have final say in the game plan that will be used against that upcoming opponent. The main duty of the pro scout is to follow certain teams all season to learn everything possible about their tendencies on offense, defense, and special teams. Then, when the next game was against one of those teams, to "sell" the coaches (Noll, George Perles, and Woody Widenhofer) on the specific plays and defense that should be employed that week. Coach Noll assigned me division opponents Cleveland, Houston, and Cincinnati, teams the Steelers would play twice. Back then, there were only 14 games in the season and I would be involved in the six most important. Win all the division games and it is very likely you will win the division, thus making it into the playoffs.

I was thrilled. I said to myself that I must have done a lot better in the interview than I thought. Then one day, one of the other coaches explained to me that because the Steelers had such a long history of preparing to play those teams, they would instantly know if I was giving them bad advice. Another shot to my confidence.

Being an Emerald, Coach Noll emphasized organization, structure, and fundamentals. He was not a rah-rah guy and seldom gave pre-game speeches. He always seemed totally focused and dead serious in every interaction I had with him. Half the time, I was not even sure he knew my name. There were never any pleasantries exchanged and no real attempt to build a relationship. It was all predicated on what I could bring him that would give the Steelers an edge. Being a Ruby, I was fine without the relationship, but I struggled to learn the proper way to get Chuck to adopt what I "knew" would work. With him, everything had to be proved in a methodical, analytical way. Something it took me half the season to learn to do.

In the end, here is what Coach Noll was about and what he taught me regarding the Emerald Style:

- Work hard, prepare diligently, and good things will happen.
- Be humble, keep a low profile, and let the players have the glory.
- Be at meetings on time and do your job. Let the people take care of what they are responsible for.
- If you make a mistake one time, you now have a history, because one time creates a history.
- Any single player on a team can derail it, so everyone is important no matter how minimal their role might appear to be.
- A championship team starts with great players but they must follow the direction of one person – and everyone knew who that one person was. Chuck paid attention to the smallest of details but seemed to do so without micromanaging.
- Football teaches humility because if you rest on your laurels, it does not take long for someone to surpass you and knock you off your perch.
- When Chuck said, "How are you?" he did not really want to know.

The Sapphire Style

The most powerful traits of Sapphires are their preference for building relationships and helping others. They are usually friendly, approachable, and supportive. They love working in teams. They tend to possess natural coaching skills and value other people's feelings, ideas, and goals. The vast majority of Sapphires are extroverts.

The number one motivator for a Sapphire is helping the team succeed. They pride themselves as being known as the glue that holds the team together or the straw that stirs the drink. They have patience and work very hard to make relationships work.

On the downside, Sapphires dislike interpersonal conflicts with their boss and peers so much that they often quit organizations if these conflicts cannot be quickly resolved. In stressful situations, they often either say nothing or say what others want to hear. Sapphires are not very skilled at self-promotion, as they hope that their boss and peers will recognize their accomplishments. They are uncomfortable disagreeing with others and often withhold their true feelings, preferring to not make waves.

In leadership positions, Sapphires are apt to be permissive, easily intimidated by strong people, and move way too slowly for the taste of Rubies. They can be naïve as to others' motivations, especially political motives. And, they can get overly emotional about things others would consider to be minor. They may spend too much time seeking consensus or the approval of their boss before taking action.

The Sapphire Style gravitates to careers in customer service, employee relations, teaching, counseling, community service, nursing, environmental sciences, and the arts. While 40 percent of people in the general population are Sapphires, only 10 percent of managers are Sapphires.

A Quick Guide to the Sapphire Style

Positive Traits	Negative Traits
Approachable	Dependent
Empathetic	Slow-Paced
Good Listener	Easily Intimidated
Cooperative	Difficulty with Conflict
Loyal	Permissive
Team Players	Naïve
Give Non-Judgmental Support	Over-Personalize Criticism

Influencing Sapphires

- Ask for their opinions, involvement, and ideas.
- Allow them time for socializing.
- Show Sapphires how they can help the team.
- Do not yell at or intimidate them.
- Share personal insights and your background with them.
- Allow them to work in teams.
- Make frequent eye contact, smile readily, and call Sapphires by name.
- Do not overload them with data.
- Do things to break the ice.
- Tell personal stories or anecdotes to warm up your message.
- Try and create the feeling that you and they are working jointly to resolve a problem vs. selling them something.

Suggestions for Sapphires when Interacting with Rubies

- Be more forceful than you are comfortable with being.
- Do not waste a lot of time trying to build the relationship.
- Do not procrastinate in decision-making.
- Be candid in your critiques.
- Be specific about what you think – no waffling.
- Try and keep from getting emotional.

- Replace "I better not" with "I'll take a chance."
- Don't take it personally when Rubies push you. It is their way of seeing if you have conviction.

Suggestions for Sapphires when dealing with Emeralds

- Be more thoroughly prepared for meetings.
- Do not waste a lot of time trying to build a relationship.
- Use data, facts, and logic and cut out the emotion.
- Give Emeralds time to think and get their questions answered.
- Do not invade their personal space by touching them or standing too close.
- Emphasize your credentials and track record.

Famous People Who Exhibit the Sapphire Style

None of the following people have been assessed on the Interpersonal Preferences Profile, but each seem to exhibit many of the characteristics associated with the Sapphire Style.

- Tony Dungy – Former Head Coach, Super Bowl Champion, Indianapolis Colts
- Sarah Palin – Former Governor, State of Alaska
- S. Truett Cathy – Founder, Chick-fil-A restaurants
- Jenny Craig – Founder, Jenny Craig
- Mary Kay Ash – Founder, Mary Kay, Inc.
- Jim Caldwell – Head Coach, Detroit Lions
- Lori Greiner – Serial entrepreneur and host of TV show *Shark Tank*
- Sheri McCoy – CEO, Avon
- Barbara Walters – Talk Show Host

Tales from the Workplace

When you think of a friendly, approachable, supportive Sapphire who loves to help others, a 5'11" 255-pound battering ram NFL running back would probably not be the first person who would come to mind. But it might if you knew former Pittsburgh Steelers Hall of Famer Jerome Bettis.

Jerome, nicknamed "The Bus" because of his history of carrying 2-3 defenders on his back on the way to the end zone, is one of the most beloved players in league history. He played thirteen seasons rushing for 13,662 yards (fifth in NFL history) and 91 touchdowns. As impressive as these on-field accomplishments are, his teammates revered him for being the glue that held the team together season after season.

In early 1996 the St. Louis Rams were looking to trade Bettis after only three years with the team. Players drafted in the first round (10th overall) who were named offensive rookie of the year do not normally find themselves on the trading block. The Pittsburgh Steelers seldom trade their high-round draft picks for established players but hearing that Bettis was available intrigued them. But in their minds there had to be something wrong. Why would the Rams want to get rid of their best running back? Was he injured? Did he have a drug problem (in his youth Jerome reportedly admitted to having sold crack cocaine)? Was he a cancer in the locker room? Did he alienate the coaching staff?

At the time, I was doing some one-on-one sports coaching with a couple of the Steelers stars. I had come to be known by a few folks in the General Managers office. They asked me to delve into the matter and do an assessment to see what the true story was regarding Bettis.

To make a long story short, my assessment turned up that Jerome was perfectly healthy. The coaching staff thought he was a "Boy Scout." His teammates universally loved him. And far from dealing drugs, Bettis was an active crusader in his hometown of Detroit giving speeches to gang members on the evils of drugs. As it turned out, it was simple why the Rams no longer wanted him. New coach Rich Brooks was installing a passing oriented offense based upon speed and Jerome's smash mouth style of play was no longer a fit.

So, on April 20, 1996, the Steelers pulled off one of the great steals in NFL history by trading their second and fourth round draft picks to St. Louis in exchange for Bettis and a third round draft pick.

The Fire Opal Style (Strong Combination of Ruby with Sapphire)

The most powerful trait of the Fire Opal Style is their desire to compete while preserving relationships. They tend to be participative leaders who use a consultative style of decision-making. This inclusive approach resonates with both Generation X and Millennials, as these generations do not like the idea of superior/subordinate forms of leadership.

Most Fire Opals are seen by others as charismatic and highly persuasive. In sports, they are referred to as "player's coaches." People seem to love giving them their best effort because Fire Opals include them and take time to build a relationship on a personal level. Fire Opals are often savvy politically. Instead of being turned off by an organization's political side, they flourish by learning to succeed within the system.

On the downside, Fire Opals are often seen as manipulative – whether they mean to be or not. People can view their attempts to build relationships as disingenuous – a means to achieve the goal the Fire Opal intends to meet. Their biggest weakness is their tendency to make consequential decisions impulsively. They tend to frustrate others by exaggerating, and through frequent changes in decisions or direction once data that was skipped is presented.

Fire Opals gravitate to careers in high level executive positions in very large companies, politicians, non-technical sales, public relations managers, litigation attorneys, marketing managers, and sales managers. Fire Opals comprise about 10 percent of the general population and account for 15 percent of people in managerial roles.

A Quick Guide to the Fire Opal Style

Positive Traits	Negative Traits
Participative	Manipulating
Democratic	Impulsive
Charismatic	Overly Emotional
Persuasive	Exaggerates
Tactful	Breaks Confidences
Savvy Politically	Over Protects His/Her Group

Influencing Fire Opals

- Support their vision or dreams.
- Interact in an approachable manner.
- Be energetic and moderately emotional.
- Take their tendency to embellish things in stride.
- Be willing to share real problems with them.
- Do not be turned off by their political maneuvering.
- Move quickly and forcefully.
- Help them become grounded in reality. Let them know what it will take to make their vision come to fruition without seeming to be negative or a "buzz kill."

Suggestions for Fire Opals when interacting with Emeralds

- Constantly guard against your naturally impulsive tendencies.
- Acquire and present more data than you otherwise would.
- Recognize the tendency to protect your group may actually impede or interfere with the work of other groups.

- Treat confidences people share with you as akin to "attorney client privilege."
- Realize Emeralds will not appreciate your rushed approach. They will likely feel they are being manipulated.
- Watch your emotional level. Your Ruby preference may cause you to lash out impulsively while your Sapphire tendency may cause you to choke up or tear up at inappropriate times. Learn to feel these emotions coming on and learn to control them.

Famous People Who Exhibit the Fire Opal Style

None of the following people have been assessed on the Interpersonal Preferences Profile, but each seem to exhibit many of the characteristics associated with the Fire Opal Style.

- Ronald Reagan – President of the United States
- Bill Clinton – President of the United States
- Barack Obama – President of the United States
- Dr. Martin Luther King, Jr. – Civil Rights Activist
- Pete Carroll – Head Coach, Super Bowl Champion, Seattle Seahawks
- Mike Tomlin – Head Coach, Super Bowl Champion, Pittsburgh Steelers
- Marissa Mayer – CEO, Yahoo
- Jeff Immelt – CEO, General Electric
- Indra Nooyi – CEO, PepsiCo
- Robert K. Kraft – Owner, New England Patriots
- Earvin "Magic" Johnson – Hall of Fame Basketball Player

Tales from the Workplace

Michelle Vargas, Director, Human Resources at NFP, an employee benefits consulting firm in Orem, Utah, embodies all that is right with the Fire Opal style. She is charismatic, personable, intelligent, and highly persuasive. People love her because she is authentic and takes the time to build relationships on a personal level. She balances these characteristics with a missionary zeal to see the organization succeed and by acting as the consummate professional at all times.

Michelle believes that every opportunity that has come her way is a result of a helping attitude coupled with demonstrated performance. She has a service mentality regarding her clients. She sees her mission as helping to solve their problems with the minimum of red tape possible. Her customers love that she takes the time to really understand their needs and issues. Her drive to perform in ways that exceed their expectations causes them to place great trust in her.

Michelle practices the pay-it-forward concept as well as anyone I have known. She took on the role of president of her local Human Resources Chapter (and anyone who has done something similar knows what a thankless job that is). She gives of her time to serve good causes. When someone she knows calls or sends an e-mail asking for a favor, she always responds immediately, and when she can she tries to help. She believes fully in the old adage, "What goes around, comes around."

That in essence is what a Fire Opal in business is all about.

The Aquamarine Style
(Strong Combination of Emerald with Sapphire)

The most powerful trait of the Aquamarine Style is their ability to combine personal warmth with a structured, disciplined approach to work. Aquamarines are patient, calm, principled, and usually trusted by most people who get to know them.

Aquamarines like to use their minds to solve difficult problems that affect the greater good. When they encounter unethical behavior at work, they feel compelled to go public with their findings even at the possible expense of their own careers or reputation.

Aquamarines seem to have the innate ability to see both sides of arguments. They are viewed by others as fair and impartial, and thus are great at moderating disputes.

Aquamarines tend to be procrastinators, often falling behind the time curve, schedule wise. Their Sapphire side falls in love with relationships while their Emerald side wants to overkill on the accumulation of data. They are the least likely of the six styles to take risks. They prefer stable, predictable, structured ways of doing things. Aquamarines also have the most difficulty when there is conflict with the boss or within the team. They live by the famous Rodney King phrase "can't we all just get along."

The Aquamarine Style gravitates to careers as scientists in not-for-profit organizations, technical trainers, field service technicians, information technology help desk consultants, paramedics, labor arbitrators, mediators, and news anchors. In the general population, about 10 percent of people exhibit the Aquamarine Style, but only 5 percent are found in managerial positions.

A Quick Guide to the Aquamarine Style

Positive Traits	Negative Traits
Patient	Procrastinators
Calm	Difficulty with Conflict
Trusted	Risk Averse
Ethical	Noncommittal in Meetings
Predictable	Reluctant to Challenge the Rules
Practical	Overcommit, Schedule Wise
Common Sense	Frustrated by Office Politics

Influencing Aquamarines

- Do research and have your facts straight.
- Show how their work affects the greater good.
- Prove that you are worthy of their trust.
- Let them play the mediator role.
- Avoid abrupt changes in plans or direction.
- Emphasize the organization's core values.
- Do what you can to keep them on schedule.
- Allow them some time to mix with their peers.
- Deal swiftly in tackling conflicts within their team.
- Show them they will be protected if they take reasonable risks that do not work out.

Suggestions for Aquamarines when Dealing with Rubies

- Become more time efficient.
- Minimize small talk and relationship building.
- Do not overload Rubies with too much detail.
- Use milestones to assess your progress to goals so as to not get too far off track.
- Realize interpersonal or goal conflict is natural in a business setting. Don't take it personally.
- Become more realistic in your projections as to time since things seem to take longer when Aquamarines are involved.
- Understand that Rubies embrace risk. They will likely see your hesitancy to take risks as a weakness.
- Challenge systems, policies, procedures, or things that seem to make little sense. Rubies hate unnecessary waste due to mindless bureaucracy.

Famous People who Exhibit the Aquamarine Style

None of the following people have been assessed on the Interpersonal Preferences Profile, but each seem to exhibit many of the characteristics associated with the Aquamarine Style.

- Gerald Ford – President of the United States
- George H.W. Bush – President of the United States
- Mary Barra – CEO, General Motors
- Gwen Ifill – National Public Radio
- Mike McCarthy – Head Coach, Super Bowl Champion, Green Bay Packers
- Bob Schieffer – News Anchor, CBS News
- Scott Pelley – News Anchor, CBS News
- General Colin Powell – Former Secretary of State
- Phil Simms – Hall of Fame Quarterback

Tales from the Workplace

Ben Diachun, CEO of Scaled Composites runs one of the coolest companies you will ever find if you are an aerospace engineer. Scaled Composites was founded by the legendary aviation pioneer, Burt Rutan. The company's claim to fame is that it is among a very small number of places in the world where one-of-a-kind prototype aircraft are designed and built.

Ben is one of the finest people I have had the pleasure to work with in my career. He is the epitome of the humble, self-effacing, authentic leader that most of us seek to work for but seldom find. He provides a powerful example of the concept of reciprocity.

It started when Ben was a young student pilot. He was about to perform his first instrument approach in a complex airplane in bad weather. He thought out loud, "There is no way I can do this." Without missing a beat his instructor shot back, "You have the judgment, technical skills, and training to do this. I trust you to make the right decisions." The instructor saw things in Ben that he had been unable to see himself.

This pattern continued throughout Ben's career. Then one day, Burt Rutan promoted him into a leadership role much sooner than expected. Ben was surprised and not sure if he was ready to lead others. But Burt sat him down and enumerated all the qualities that he saw in him that Ben had yet to real ize he possessed. With Burt's support and coaching along the way, Ben quickly flew up the corporate ladder to now lead one of America's great institutions.

Ben adopted this same approach in leading the entire organization. He is constantly on the lookout for special talents and qualities that his people have that they might not yet see in themselves. Then reciprocating what was given to him, he helps them further develop their skills and provides ongoing guidance. He gets a thrill when his people one day realize the special gift they had all along.

Ben is not one to dwell on the negative but when I pressed him for examples of leaders he's seen who operate differently, he said the following, "Sadly, I have seen many times what happens when talented people are denied opportunity. Passionate and gifted associates approach their boss feeling they have what it takes to lead or do something. The boss shoots them down, often without explanation or justification. The results always seem to be the same. The associate becomes demoralized, disengages, the relationship with the boss becomes toxic, and they end up leaving the organization. No one wins."

The Topaz Style
(Strong Combination of Ruby with Emerald)

The most powerful trait of the Topaz Style is their ability to combine deep analysis with quick decisiveness. Topaz personalities try to apply their conceptual skills to outwit, outlast, and outplay others in competitive environments.

Topaz types are usually persevering, persistent, and demanding as bosses. They tend to abhor mediocrity. They often win through putting forth uncommon effort and cannot understand why others do not seem as dedicated as they are. They love to compete and may attempt to "win at all costs." Many end up being "workaholics."

Topaz personalities are seen by others as walking contradictions. Sometimes they move quickly and at other times tend to operate more methodically. One day, they may be up for taking a big risk, and then the next day, they may want to play it safe. On one project, they might prefer to delve into reams of data, and on other projects, they may want only surface details. Because the human mind cannot simultaneously hold such conflicting thoughts, you literally have to try and figure out if they are having a "Ruby day" or an "Emerald day."

On the downside, people who exhibit the Topaz Style tend to be the least approachable. They often come across as intimidating due to their superior intellect coupled with their forceful demeanor. They love to argue for the sake of argument, which can be frustrating to others.

Some Topaz types play a nasty game called "intellectual gotcha," where they ask a question in public that they already know the answer to, so they can pounce and show their superiority if you don't know the answer. The Topaz manager runs into trouble at work if they become too dominant or overly critical. Most Topaz types do not "read" body language, voice tone, or facial expressions accurately.

The Topaz Style gravitates to careers such as heads of high-tech companies, executive recruiters, turn-around specialists, "shock TV" personalities, investigative journalists, and crime scene investigators. In the general population, the percentage of Topaz types is only 5 percent, but they represent 10 percent of those holding managerial positions.

A Quick Guide to the Topaz Style

Positive Traits	Negative Traits
Persevering	Unapproachable
Persistent	Argumentative
Demanding	Intellectual Gotcha
Ambitious	Difficulty Reading People
Competitive	Dominating
Energetic	Critical

Influencing Topazes

- Do extensive analysis but present it quickly.
- Be forceful and demonstrate conviction.
- Try to show that you are not intimidated.
- Act professional and confident at all times.
- Allow them to be the center of attention.
- Find things about them that you can praise or compliment.
- Engage in spirited debate, but allow them the opportunity to save face when they are wrong.
- Do not over-react in a negative way to their criticism, learn from it then move on.
- Help them understand the impact of their decisions on the human element of the business.

Suggestions for Topaz when dealing with Sapphires

- Don't play "intellectual gotcha." If you need information from someone, explain why you need it before asking.
- Learn to soften your written and verbal communication. Use qualifying words such as "maybe," "occasionally," "we might," and "how would you feel."
- Develop more social sensitivity awareness. Watch a lot of movies and try to focus on tone of voice, facial expressions, and the gestures of the main characters.

- Balance your criticism with equal amounts of praise. Go out of your way to observe and comment on the things that Sapphires are doing right.
- Try holding back on sharing your point of view until the Sapphires have been heard.
- Minimize arguing about the little things. Save the debating mentality for when things are really important.
- Try to develop your ability to accommodate the Sapphire in a conflict situation. Chances are it is your least-used mode of conflict handling.
- Be patient with the Sapphire's need to socialize and use social media such as Facebook, Twitter, and Instagram at work. Remember that you hired Sapphires for their social skills and if their social needs are frustrated, you will lose the special qualities you recruited.

Famous People who Exhibit the Topaz Style

None of the following people have been assessed on the Interpersonal Preferences Profile, but each seem to exhibit many of the characteristics associated with the Topaz Style.

- Steve Jobs – Co-Founder of Apple
- Virginia "Ginny" Rometti – CEO, IBM
- Tom Coughlin – Former Head Coach of Super Bowl Champion, New York Giants
- General James "Mad Dog" Mattis – Secretary of Defense
- Mark Hurd and Safra Catz – Co-CEOs, Oracle
- Bill Gates – Founder of Microsoft
- Bill Maher, Bill O'Reilly, and Rachel Maddow – Shock TV Personalities
- Hillary Clinton – Former Secretary of State
- Carly Fiorina – Former CEO, Hewlett Packard
- Nick Saban – Head Coach, University of Alabama Football, multiple National Champions

Tales from the Workplace

When it comes to relationships, Topaz types are a curious lot. They tend to be intensely loyal to those fortunate enough to be included in their tight-knit circle and to hell with everyone else.

Brian Burke, president of the National Hockey League (NHL) Calgary Flames and former executive vice president and general manager of the 2007 Stanley Cup Champion Anaheim Ducks provides the perfect example. I first interviewed "Burkie" as he is known back in 2009. Critics call him tough, relentless, truculent, outspoken, and say he plays by his own rules.

There is no question that Burkie is unapologetic in his demand for excellence in everyone from the Zamboni driver to his senior executives. He has the courage to clarify expectations, even those that may be unpopular with his associates.

I will never forget Burkie getting up to speak during the 2008 welcome dinner for the Anaheim Ducks rookies. To this day his ten-minute talk is still the best clarification of expectations I have ever heard a leader deliver. His message was stern and unambiguous. In part, he said, "Our team is not run as a democracy. We expect you to follow the direction of your coach immediately and without hesitation. We demand that you play within our system and not freelance. We expect you to competently handle your role, whether it be four minutes or twenty-four minutes of ice time per game. In the off-season we expect you to volunteer a minimum of sixteen hours a week in your local community. Becoming a champion is hard, and work is not always going to be fun. The enjoyment comes from the relationships that you will build with your teammates and the winning that we will all enjoy together."

Burkie used an interesting analogy with the players to make his point. He said, "A hockey team operates a lot like a symphony orchestra. Center stage up front is the first chair violinist. She is extremely talented and bathed in the spotlight. Having someone like that is critical to the symphony. But also important are the tubas and French horns in the rear. Everyone must accept their defined roles for the whole orchestra to produce a beautiful sound. All the musicians need to follow one person's direction. And from the conductor's standpoint, he cannot lead people who do not want to be part of the team."

Despite Burkie's tough exterior, few outsiders ever get to see the relationship building and intense loyalty that he has to his inner circle. Calgary Flames captain Mark Giordano says of Burkie, "He always has your back as a player. It feels like whatever you need he will be on your side." Flames player Joe Colborne, who was also with Burkie when both were with the Toronto Maple Leaf organization says, "He is someone I feel I can talk to anytime I need counsel. I have so much respect for him." To a man the players all have similar comments about Burkie.

If Burkie sees one of his people wronged, he intervenes. When Dennis Wideman was handed a 20-game suspension by the NHL for colliding with an official, Burkie flew to league headquarters to stand up for his player. Everyone sees Burkie roaming around the facility, hanging out, and growing relationships. "With Burkie, it is not management you never see. We know that he cares deeply for us as people, not just as players"

Recognizing the Behavioral Style of Others

With practice, you can become surprisingly adept at predicting the interpersonal style of others simply by focusing on three main indicators – speed, directive behavior, and emotional control.

Speed

Rubies love a fast-paced and multi-tasking environment. They give others the impression that time is of the essence and that they have many other things to get to during the day. They check their watch frequently and in meetings will often send text messages or e-mails on subjects unrelated to the meeting. When others are presenting data to them, Rubies will likely flip several pages ahead or cut the presenter short. Many Rubies have nervous mannerisms such as shaking their legs under the table, doodling, or tapping their fingers. Above all, Rubies like to minimize small talk and get into the subject matter at hand quickly.

By contrast, Sapphires, Emeralds, and Aquamarines prefer a much slower pace at work. Sapphires take time for ice breakers, engage in non-work-related conversations, and attempt to build relationships before diving into work. They may spend time at the water cooler chit chatting or on Twitter, Instagram, Facebook, or LinkedIn.

Emeralds take time to gather and analyze data. They move at a methodical, measured pace. They tend to freeze under intense time pressure. Aquamarines do a bit of both relationship building and data gathering. Fire Opals and Topaz types are comfortable at a moderate pace.

A Quick Guide to SPEED at Work

Slow	Moderate	Fast
Sapphire	Fire Opal	Ruby
Emerald	Topaz	
Aquamarine		

Directive Behavior

Rubies love to be in control and tend to get uncomfortable when they are not in charge. In a meeting, Rubies are usually the first ones to make a statement or grab a marker and start drawing on a white board. They are kind of like the dog that pees everywhere to carve out their turf. Subliminally, they are sending a message that they are in charge.

When Rubies make their points, they often do so emphatically and may even pound the table. They share their opinion readily and forcefully on virtually any subject even if they only have a thimbleful of knowledge on the topic. Rubies compete with others to attempt to get their way and are often disappointed if their view did not prevail.

On the other hand, Sapphires, Emeralds, and Aquamarines are less directive. They tend to ask questions of others before sharing their thoughts on a subject. A great way to tell a Sapphire from an Emerald is by paying attention to the type of questions they ask. Emeralds tend to ask objective, data-oriented questions, such as what you *think* and what you can *prove*.

Sapphires often ask questions about more personal and subjective things. They want to know how you *feel*.

Sapphires, Emeralds, and Aquamarines can take control of meetings, but have no problem deferring when others like to lead. They usually present their views in a more cautious, tentative manner. They soften the blow with qualifiers like "I am on the fence on this, how do you see it" or "I am leaning in this direction but can be swayed."

A Quick Guide to Directive Behavior at Work

Non-Directive	Moderate	Directive
Sapphire	Fire Opal	Ruby
Emerald	Topaz	
Aquamarine		
Risk Averse		Risk Taker
Tentative		Emphatic
Goes Along		Takes Initiative
Asks Questions		Opinionated
Reserved		Active
Cooperative		Competitive
Low Need to Control		High Need to Control

Emotional Control

Rubies, Emeralds, and Topazes tend to be somewhat non-emotional at work. They prefer to tackle the task at hand instead of spending time building the relationship. They can be hard to read facially and usually do not wear their emotions on their sleeves. Extreme Emeralds speak in a monotone voice.

Sapphires tend to be very emotional. They love conversation. You can see pain, anger, frustration, and inquisitiveness on their face. They share their feelings readily. When someone asks how they are doing, Sapphires think others really want to know and may give startlingly frank answers.

Recently, I rode on an airplane from Orange County, California, to Salt Lake City. The flight was less than an hour and a half long. As a Ruby, I did not want a "relationship" with my seat mate. I wanted to get to Salt Lake City in the most productive way possible. So, I did not make eye contact with the woman sitting next to me. I had my headset on listening to music with my book open underlining significant passages.

Out of the corner of my eye, I saw the woman sitting next to me is a Sapphire. How did I know this? Well, before taking off, she was kneeling in her seat talking to strangers in the row behind us. When she had to buckle in for the flight, that was when I got nervous. She apparently did not bring anything to read or a device to listen to music. A Sapphire in such a situation can only go about 10 minutes without conversation, and I kid you not, she turned to me with a big smile and with one hand took an earmuff off the headset from my head and with the other hand closed my book, saying, "Hi, I'm Sue, who are you?" For the next hour, I spent the flight trying to politely get back to my work to no avail. It was like the classic scene from the movie *Planes, Trains and Automobiles*, where Sapphire shower curtain ring salesman John Candy continually interrupts Ruby business executive Steve Martin.

A Quick Guide to Emotional Control

Emotional	Moderate	Non-Emotional
Sapphires	Aquamarine	Ruby
	Fire Opal	Emerald
		Topaz

Enjoy Conversation	Task Oriented
Easy to Read	Hard to Read
Shares Feelings	Little Sharing of Feelings
Animated Facial Expressions	Somewhat Expressionless

A Person's Office is Often a Clue to Their Style

While not as predictive as speed, directive behavior, or emotional control, a person's work space is frequently quite telling about their style.

A Ruby office will project power, ego, and or efficiency. Typically, there are pictures with important people, certificates, plaques, medals, trophies, or models of the company's products. The piles on their desks will be organized with the one thing most important they are working on in the center of the desk. Higher level executives will often have expensive artwork, an informal setting area with a butler's table, and a credenza with lamps behind the desk.

A Sapphire office will feel warm and friendly. There will be photos of the family, kindergarten drawings of kids and grandkids, warm colors, and plants. The Sapphire will often come out from behind the desk to sit side by side.

The Emerald office can look one of two ways. The organized Emerald will have Gantt charts, spreadsheets, and neatly stacked piles. The absent-minded professor Emerald will have white boards filled with scribbles and seemingly disorganized piles of stuff everywhere.

Dress Can Also be an Indicator

Emeralds tend to dress in much the same way as you would expect given what their office looks like. The absent-minded professor Emeralds really do not pay much attention at all to their clothes. Things may not match, and you certainly will not see what they wear in *Vogue* or *GQ Magazine*. The organized Emerald will usually have a much understated style of dress. Things match, hair is perfect, and they do not come off at all pretentious or showy.

Sapphires like to dress comfortable and casual. In the holiday season, they may wear sweaters that others would consider goofy. They often use dress as a way to create a personal signature look with hats, scarves, jackets, sweaters, and shoes that say "I am hip" or "I am a non –conformist."

Rubies tend to dress for prestige. They prefer designer labels such as Ralph Lauren, power suits, silk ties, high end purses, designer shoes, and expensive accessories.

Adjusting to the Preferences of Others

Once you have a pretty good assessment of the interpersonal preferences of another person, you can dramatically increase that person's comfort with you. I have found through my association with, and study of, effective leaders and top salespeople, that a high percentage of the most successful ones spend a great deal of time consciously or unconsciously altering or adjusting their own style to better meet the needs of others. What they do in effect is to *temporarily* subvert their own comfortable style and adopt characteristics associated with the style they are trying to "match." This "matching process" makes the person doing the adjusting a bit, to a great deal, uncomfortable. But this has the effect of putting the person they are interacting with at ease. The hope is that by treating a person as he/she desires to be treated, the leader, or salesperson, can more readily accomplish the goal he/she is trying to reach. This occurs because the other person does not experience as much stress or frustration with the leader, or salesperson, as he/she would if no adjustments or accommodations were made.

By contrast, I have also noticed that less-effective people in leadership or sales positions tend to act in a manner that is comfortable for them regardless of the effect their style has upon others. Basically, they make little or no attempt to match the style preferences and behavioral expectations of other people. The result is often a great deal of tension or frustration in the relationship, which gets in the way of achieving their ultimate goal.

Tales from the Workplace

Bob Dobbs, Vice President of Great American Financial in Cincinnati, has taken on many challenging assignments over the years outside of the company. One such challenge was leading a task force at his Alma Mater, the University of Cincinnati (UC), to combine the fundraising activities of two separate entities, the UC Alumni Association and the UC Foundation. The assignment was thought to be so difficult that Bob's closest friends said, "He must be dumber than dog crap to take this on."

Removing one of the most important functions, fundraising, from one entity and transferring full responsibility for the activity into another standalone and sometimes competing body without diminishing the viability of the "losing" organization is a complicated process fraught with potential pitfalls. There are egos at stake and turf that members of the Board feel they have a fiduciary responsibility to protect. The proper legal hoops have to be jumped through. So according to Bob, the key was finding a way to get buy-in. His group could not command it to happen, and they did not have the power to force it to happen. Members of both Boards had to be convinced that it was in the best interest of the University for there to be one focal point of contact with the potential donor.

Following are some of the key elements that factored into Bob and his team successfully accomplishing the goal.

1. <u>Research</u>. The task force set out to see if there were other universities that had faced and overcome the same challenge, and if so, what could be learned from their success. Fortunately, there was precedent at two similar size universities, the University of Wisconsin and the Ohio State University.

2. <u>Network</u>. Bob had previously served as President of the UC Alumni Association and through that knew many members of the current Alumni Board. In addition, he had contacts throughout the University. He felt that a "disinterested third party" who could challenge the groups thinking might be a great addition to the task force. Bob asked the Dean of the College Conservatory of Music to play that role in his group.

   Because Bob was on the current UC Board of Trustees, he was able to tap into that network as well. He sought out members of both boards and met with them one on one to get their ideas and assess their level of concern.

3. <u>Create a Shared Vision.</u> Bob instinctively realized that the best way to get everyone involved and to put their parochial interests aside was through the creation of a powerful collective vision. He had an ace up his sleeve in that each board member was highly interested in the University, since they had voluntarily chosen to take a leadership role without monetary compensation. Bob's team crafted a vision of how the best interests of the University could be more effectively served through having a single fundraising arm. The vision was then sold using Ruby, Emerald, and Sapphire "hooks" that tapped into the "buying motives" of each board member in a very personal way.

4. <u>Ego Protection.</u> Bob and his team realized that those who stood to lose the most were the board members of the UC Alumni Association. They were being

stripped of a major reason for their existence. So, the group decided to create a standing committee of the Board of Trustees that would include every member of the Alumni Association Board. Now they could say they proudly served on _two_ important groups of the University.

The Price of Adjusting to Others' Preferences

In the classic movie, *A League of Their Own*, Tom Hanks plays the very Ruby manager of a women's professional softball team during World War II. Early on, a Sapphire outfielder named Evelyn throws the ball to the wrong base. In typical Ruby fashion, Hanks runs out to confront Evelyn in front of her teammates. He gets in her face and says, "You are throwing the ball to the wrong base and your error is killing this team." In the midst of his tirade, Evelyn starts to cry. Hanks responds, "Are you crying, are you crying? There is no crying in baseball, no crying." Because Hanks did not understand that Evelyn was a Sapphire who does not take a frontal assault of criticism well, she does not even hear him and thus does not change her behavior.

Later in the movie, it is evident that Hanks has grown in sophistication as a leader. When Evelyn once again throws the ball to the wrong base, he uses a much softer approach. As he charges out onto the field with his fists clenched, you can see the frustration that has built up inside of him and you know what he wants to do. However, as Evelyn cautiously approaches Hanks expecting another fusillade of anger, it dawns on him that this approach did not work very well the first time around. Instead of lashing out, Hanks takes a deep breath, unclenches his fists, looks Evelyn in the eyes, smiles, and calmly says, "Now Evelyn, you are still throwing the ball to the wrong base. That is something you and I need to work on before next season." Evelyn reciprocates with a smile, nods her head, and says, "Okay." Point made, she at least heard him this time around. But, as Hanks turns away from Evelyn with the camera still on him, he begins to tense up and shake violently. The stress that Evelyn once felt in her body has been transferred to Hanks. This adjustment was terribly difficult for him to do because it goes against the grain of who he is. But by focusing on what he wanted to accomplish, he has a greater chance of getting a much better result.

Influencing a "Mixed" Audience

Trying to influence others in a meeting where each of the various styles of people are present is obviously more difficult. One strategy is to focus the bulk of your presentation to whom you perceive to be the key decision-maker. The risk in this approach is that there may be others who are very influential to the key decision-maker that you are unaware of, and who may negatively influence that person after the fact.

Another somewhat safer strategy would be to hit all three core "buying" motives – Ruby, Emerald, and Sapphire. The question is, in what order do you hit these motives?

Rubies tend to have the shortest attention span, so it is important to get to them quickly. Be fast, forceful, and get to the bottom line expeditiously. Stroke their ego a bit in the process. Make it clear that you value what they value and that they will have the final say.

Next, hit the Emerald theme. They are the natural skeptics and they may see you as just another "hip shooter" with no data. Emphasize degrees, credentials, track record, and the extensive research that you have done. Make it clear that each of the options you present have strengths and limitations and let them know the things that have been done to reduce risk.

Finally, engage the Sapphires. They usually want the relationship to work so they will hang with you the longest. Smile, make frequent eye contact, call them by name, and involve them to the extent you can in a dialogue.

During the first few minutes of your presentation, pay close attention to facial expressions and body language of your audience to help you gauge whether you are going too fast or too slow, presenting too much data or not enough, and are relating well or poorly. Then adjust accordingly. Visualize yourself as a juggler. You have Ruby, Emerald, and Sapphire gems you are juggling. You win if no gem hits the floor.

CHAPTER 3

※

STRATEGY 2 – DEVELOP EXCELLENCE IN THE 8 CORE COMPETENCIES OF HIGHLY INFLUENTIAL PEOPLE

"Good habits are hard to form but easy to live with.
Bad habits are easy to form but hard to live with."

Brian Tracy

UNDERSTANDING THE SIX Interpersonal Styles and making a conscious effort to adapt one's own style to meet the needs of others is an excellent starting point in building more productive relationships. But to become truly exceptional interpersonally requires insight into and the discipline to develop the eight core competencies of highly influential people.

- Emotional Control
- Awareness
- Social Comfort
- Social Sensitivity
- Executive Presence
- Flexibility
- Confident Body Language
- Effective Conflict Handling

Emotional Control

Emotional outbursts at work are a sign of immaturity at the very least, and if they continue over time can lead to hostile work environment lawsuits. A couple of decades ago, it was still acceptable for a CEO to fling a binder across a boardroom table at an underling whose presentation failed to inspire. They may have even been able to blister Wall Street analysts on a conference call who downgraded their stock. Today, leaders who "lose it" in a public forum are often out of a job by the next sunrise.

Sure, we all blow our stack on occasion, but maintaining our composure when we are upset should be the norm. I am not saying that leaders have to be like Spock from *Star Trek*, totally devoid of emotion. After all, a certain amount of passion can make points more dramatically and it tends to highlight the degree of importance one places on things. What I am talking about is developing the ability to discuss issues without becoming angry and learning to accept criticism in a non-defensive manner.

Tales from the Workplace

A few years ago, I was in the middle of a three-hour assessment of an executive for a half-million dollar per year job with an NFL team. He had an incredible set of educational credentials, an impressive resume for an up and coming young man, and he had already passed muster in previous interviews with the owner and three other team executives.

For the first ninety minutes of our interview, his answers to questions were vague, incomplete, and often filled with hyperbole. Since there were still ninety minutes left, I decided to level with him. I casually mentioned that I was having difficulty making an assessment on the areas I had covered and in the interest of giving him the fairest possible shot at the job, that I would appreciate a bit more depth and specificity in his responses.

To my shock, he got red in the face, slammed his briefcase on the boardroom table, and said the interview was over. He then proceeded to launch into an expletive-filled monologue about the organization. He evidently concluded that my request meant that he had already lost the job instead of giving him the best chance of success, which was my intent. He simply came apart at the seams right before my eyes. Not exactly executive timber, if you know what I mean.

When people in leadership positions lash out at underlings, bad things tend to happen. A typical response is to avoid the leader all together. Eventually the leader becomes cut off from reality. Or, lower level associates feel so much tension being around such a toxic boss that their performance and health suffer. We know that a certain amount of stress is productive and keeps people on a sharp edge, but too much stress, called distress, gets in the way of both morale and performance. Lower level associates often spend a great deal of time looking for clues as to the leader's mindset by paying close attention to both verbal and non-verbal emotional signals. So, at times, it may be to the leader's benefit to mask his/her true feelings.

Psychologist Daniel Goleman, in his breakthrough book *Emotional Intelligence*, gives great insight into three of our most common emotions – anger, worry, and depression. As for anger, Goleman noted, "A life without passion would be a wasteland of neutrality, cut off and isolated from the richness of life itself. But as Aristotle observed, what is wanted is *appropriate* emotion, feelings proportionate to the circumstance."

Researchers have concluded that because of the way our brain is designed we have little control of *when* we will be swept up by emotion or *what* the emotion will be, but we can control *how long* our emotions will last.[1]

Psychologist Diane Tice in her research on dealing with anger found that it is the mood people are least skilled at controlling. Dr. Tice concluded there are three techniques that work to break the cycle of anger once it has occurred. She found that it is actually okay to get angry as long as there is roughly comparable balance with the times when we are joyous. So, one solution is to add a lot of fun activities into our lives.

A second technique that has proven to be effective is relaxation techniques such as deep breathing, yoga, meditation, soothing music, or simply walking away to cool off. Perhaps the most potent technique is reframing. We can try tamping down our anger by showing mercy. Say you are driving a car on the interstate and some jerk comes flying by going twenty miles per hour faster than you and swerves into your lane, narrowly missing the front of your car. Instead of what would be our normal reaction of getting angry, yelling (even though the driver cannot hear us), and flipping them the finger (even though they are now too far ahead to see it), we can reframe how we think about the incident. We could say to ourselves, "Perhaps he had a medical emergency or maybe he did not realize how close he came to me."

Then there is calculated anger. The kind that causes outrage when we see an injustice. This type of anger is not only fine, it is healthy as long as we do not perceive injustice everywhere we look. For instance, most of us know people who see everything as "racist" even though a specific act may have had no discriminatory intent at all. Calculated anger directed at the right things can make us powerful.[2]

The current poster child for lack of emotional control is the supremely talented yet mercurial star wide receiver of the New York Giants, Odell Beckham, Jr. The first incident occurred on December 20, 2015, when he completely lost his cool. Carolina Panthers star defensive back Josh Norman (a bit of a hothead himself) had frustrated Beckham for the better part of the game. Near the end of the game, OBJ as he is known, launched a violent cheap shot at the head of Norman.

In a much-awaited rematch with Norman, now with the Washington Redskins on September 25, 2016, OBJ wigged out after his quarterback Eli Manning tossed a careless interception. This time he vented his rage by smashing a kicking net on the sidelines.

By now you may have heard about OBJ and his wide receiver buddies chartering a plane, flying to Miami, and partying on a yacht with Justin Beiber and Trey Songz on their day off the week before a critical playoff game against the Green Bay Packers. This caused a media feeding frenzy and provided a major distraction to the team.

On January 8, 2017, after one of the most dismal performances of his career and a loss to the Packers, OBJ reportedly beat his head into his locker and punched a hole in the wall of the clubhouse at Lambeau Field.

Granted, football is game of emotion and there is nothing wrong with being a person who plays with passion. But when this immature behavior becomes a distraction to the rest of the organization, it is time to grow up.

Dr. Goleman also shed some light on the opposite mood of anger, which is depression. To remedy depression, most people do the two worst things possible – drink alcohol and isolate themselves. Alcohol is a depressant and will only add to a depressed state. And when people isolate themselves from others, they tend to wallow in their misery, mentally replaying the causes of their depression.

Dr. Goleman recommends two strategies for dealing with depression. First is to get your mind off of the depressing thoughts by doing exciting things with positive people. Attend a sporting event (or play sports yourself), see a funny movie (avoid tearjerkers), go to a concert, read an uplifting book, volunteer to do charity work, or go to the Improv. Each of these things will lift your mood or at the very least distract you from your depressing thoughts. Do something, even if it is as simple as finishing a chore or getting dressed up.

Reframing also works with depression. Say your lover unexpectedly breaks up with you. That type of event sends many people into an emotional tailspin. Try and look at the situation differently. Focus on times where the relationship was not at all that pleasant and try and see all the signs that may have indicated that he or she was not the right person for you.

Another aspect of emotional control that haunts many leaders is worry. Consultant John Narciso calls worry "suffering in advance." Of course, worry does have a positive side, in that it might alert us for the need to do things, which might head off or solve an impending problem. Worry becomes problematic when it is chronic.

The key to effectively dealing with chronic worrying is to catch ourselves heading into worry mode quickly before we become consumed by it, then challenge ourselves with a healthy dose of skepticism. "Is it probable the event will even occur?" "Does it really help to keep running through what might happen over and over?"[3]

A Quick Guide to Improving Emotional Control

- Realize that when you are criticized, there is probably a grain of truth somewhere in that criticism. Look for what might be true.
- Pause and take a deep breath when you feel anger coming on. Do isometrics. Focus on a pleasant memory or simply walk away until you have calmed down.
- Consider the source when people get under your skin. Do you really care what some people think of you? Why?
- Pretend that you are in a high-stakes poker game with everyone looking at your every gesture. Practice hard at keeping your facial expressions as neutral as possible. It does get easier with practice.
- Enlist a trusted friend or colleague to tell you when your gestures do not seem to match your words.
- Follow the sound advice of Dr. Daniel Goleman and Dr. Diane Tice listed above.

Awareness

Have you ever noticed how some people just seem to be "plugged in" to everything going on around them while others seem somewhat oblivious? According to the renowned sport psychologist, Dr. Robert Nideffer, who has spent a lifetime studying how people "pay attention," much of one's "attentional style" is programmed into us pre-birth.

According to Dr. Nideffer, our brains are wired to pay attention three ways – Aware, Focused, and Conceptual. People pre-disposed to be high in awareness seem to easily and correctly read the non-verbal cues of others. They tend to almost instinctively know the things that motivate others to do their best. They seem to notice what people wear, how their work space is organized, and hear sounds that others block out.

People who are more focused are just the opposite. They misread or do not even notice other people's voice tone, body language, or facial expressions. They do, however, have an uncanny ability to lock onto something, block out most external stimuli, and move steadily toward their goals. Conceptually wired people tend to spend a lot of their energy bouncing things off the top of their heads internally. They are usually much less aware than the average person and have a hard time staying focused.

While it is possible to develop skill in all three attentional areas, most of us start out with a strong tendency or preference for one over the other two. And without conscious effort to develop our weaker preferences, we often suffer because all three "attentional styles" are valuable at certain times.

As a leader, developing awareness can be critical the higher up the organizational ladder we climb. Senior-level executives need to be able to walk into a meeting and sense its level of effectiveness quickly. They need to be able to see trends in their business or industry well before others. And they need to know the pulse of their organization. Awareness is also necessary to create both a "vision" for the company and a vibrant "culture" that will allow the vision some chance of becoming reality.

A Quick Guide to Increasing Awareness

- Watch people's faces intently for their reaction to things you say. If you sense you may have hurt someone's feelings, make a quick recovery by saying something positive or offering an apology.
- Learn the Interpersonal Preferences Model well enough to teach it to others. It can be very helpful in your understanding of human motivation.
- Try to be honest in assessing other people's strengths and limitations. Rarely are others as skilled or unskilled as you think they are when you first meet them. Most of us tend to overestimate the skills of people we like and underestimate those of people we dislike.
- Watch critically acclaimed movies and focus on the non-verbal cues that are so important to truly understand the characters the actors are playing. Often the non-verbal signals are the truest indication of a person's feelings.
- When you walk into someone's work space, try to avoid a laser-like focus on them. Pay attention to what is on the walls and the general "feel" of the place.
- In meetings, periodically detach from the content of the meeting for a few seconds and scan the others' faces, listen to their voice tone, and watch their body language. Observe the general pace, ebb, and flow. Chances are you will see things your more-focused colleagues miss. I call this "Rising to the Press Box." The game looks much different in any arena from the ground level than it does from the Press Box level and so will the meeting.

Tales from the Workplace

To become truly motivated to increase awareness usually requires that we realize that compared to others we may not be very aware.

Many years ago, my employer sent a consultant and me to Edmonton Alberta, Canada, to conduct an audit of their largest manufacturing facility in the country and make a recommendation to either keep or terminate the employment of the facility general manager. We landed in Edmonton and the temperature was -44 degrees Fahrenheit. With some reluctance on my part, the consultant was able to persuade me to go with him to the facility that afternoon on a Sunday when no one was around except the security guard.

Honestly, I spent the hour walking the facility much like a tourist would, admiring the immense scale of the products made in this nearly million-square-foot building. As we exited the facility walking toward our car, the consultant turned to me and said, "I've seen all I need to see, I recommend termination." With what must have been a dumbfounded look on my face, I said, "How can you make such an assessment, we haven't even interviewed anyone yet?" He replied, "Oh this is one of the most out-of-control facilities I have ever seen." Sensing that I didn't get it, he said, "Let's go back in, and I will show you what I saw."

Once back inside the factory, the consultant asked me, "What is the temperature in here?" I said that I had no idea. He pointed to a thermometer that read 72 degrees Fahrenheit. I asked him what his point was. He then asked me when the last time anyone but the guard was in the building. Once again, I said that I did not know. He pointed to a time clock and said the last person punched out at 6:35 p.m. Friday. Then he said, "Since the next shift does not start until 7:00 a.m. Monday, the extreme heat necessary to keep a million-square-foot building at 72 degrees was all money literally going through the roof."

The consultant then proceeded to show me foreign object debris (FOD), unlabeled parts bins, incorrectly labeled bins, piles of scrap laying around, correctly labeled bins with three different parts where there should have only been one type of part, disorganized work stations, safety hazards, etc. In short, over fifty indicators of a terribly run operation. I had missed them all. That is the day I got "religion" so to speak and realized my awareness was generally poor. I can say with some pride, that through a lot of effort trying to become more aware, I do not miss much anymore!

Social Comfort

For lower-level leaders who supervise mainly introverted scientists, engineers, or accountants, being at ease around others may not be all that important. However, for those who aspire to higher-level positions or those who lead extroverted sales, marketing, or human resources professionals, learning to relate well with others is essential.

Like most other aspects of our personality, we are born with a predisposition toward introversion or extroversion. Some people seem quite comfortable mixing with strangers in social gatherings, while for others this might border on terrifying. You probably know people who can easily discuss their feelings and emotions with others as well as some folks who wouldn't dream of being so open. For some leaders, stopping by their associates' work space just to see how they are doing seems as natural as breathing. For other leaders, such a practice might seem uncomfortable, unnecessary, and a waste of time.

Approachability and social comfort seem to go hand in hand. Generally speaking, tall people seem less approachable than people of average height. People who seldom smile are scarier than those who smile readily. People who use self-deprecating humor seem to be more comfortable to be around than those who are somewhat humorless. Folks who are grossly overweight are often less approachable than people of average weight.

Leaders who are socially comfortable are usually accepting and trusting of others until that trust is broken, while leaders who are not comfortable in the social arena tend to be less likely to trust others. In my view, becoming more socially comfortable and approachable would seem to be wise areas to concentrate on improving for most leaders.

Tales from the Workplace

Pat Summitt, head women's basketball coach of the University of Tennessee Vols, amassed a remarkable 1,098 wins, and her teams won eight NCAA Championships during her storied career. In 2008, before she developed the debilitating early onset of Alzheimer's Disease, which would ultimately claim her life in 2016, Pat was kind enough to share a few thoughts on leadership and especially relationships with me. In Pat's own words:

"Throughout my career, people branded me as a difficult, uncaring, strict disciplinarian. Early in my first 14 years, that probably was an accurate assessment. I established hard and fast boundaries between myself and my players. I believed that if I got too close to them that I would lose my authority and objectivity. But I got that all wrong. I finally woke up and realized that through creating a deeper two-way relationship, I could better understand the strengths and weaknesses they had as players, but also how to more effectively get through to them as people. By developing a relationship based upon caring and mutual trust, I could be a better teacher and coach for them.

"I insisted that everyone call me Pat, not Coach Summitt. By my demeanor, there was never a question that I was in charge, but I wanted to let them know that I was approachable too. That while I might ride them hard in practice or during a game, I made sure they had my home phone number if they ever needed to talk. I started a practice called 'family night,' where we would all bring in photos of our life outside basketball, sit in a circle, and share elements of our past with each other. Besides the obvious benefit of having everyone develop a fuller understanding of where we had each been in life, I learned that listening to their hopes, dreams, and fears was just as important as lecturing them."

A Quick Guide to Improving Social Comfort

- Brute force is probably the best way. By this I mean, go to a lot of social events. At first this will be stressful and unpleasant. Over time, you will go from dread, to mild irritation, to somewhat enjoyable, and eventually become comfortable.
- Be the first in the room to go up to people and introduce yourself. You will have an immediate tension release as you are in control. In turn, they will also feel more comfortable with you.
- Dress casually at work once in a while, smile often, sit or kneel if you are tall, and look people in the eye. Tell a funny story about yourself. Talk about the current events of the day (avoiding religion, politics, and sex). All these things will make you more approachable.
- Learn to give people the benefit of the doubt when it comes to trusting them. Reserve healthy distrust for situations where deceit on their part would cause you more than a little inconvenience.
- Go to your associates' and peers' workspaces on occasion just to spend a minute "chatting."
- Find someone who you know has your best interests at heart and share your feelings with that person. Gradually add others to the list of people you can be open with.

Social Sensitivity

A well-known executive was sent to my Leadership Academy by the CEO of his company. I try and get as much information as I can before people attend so I can target my program to better meet the organizations' needs. The CEO said, "Basically he could follow a bull through a china shop and still manage to find some china to break, he is that abrasive." After 41 years in the business, I have come to conclude that every large organization has these insensitive, vulgar, socially inept individuals. You know the type. They send sexually or racially inappropriate e-mails to their co-workers. They tell offensive jokes at delicate times in meetings. They show a remarkable lack of tact when they give their opinion. Many talk incessantly about themselves and their conquests. Such people can create public relations or legal nightmares.

Like it or not, the world of business is still one based upon "political correctness." It is a place of zero tolerance for insensitive behavior regarding race, religion, sexual preference, or sexual harassment. One "strike" and you are out.

Consider the sad case of Helen Thomas, often called the First Lady of the Washington Press Corps. She was "dumped" into forced retirement after over fifty years of reporting because of one insensitive remark about Israel.[1] Or PGA of America President Ted Bishop, who was removed from office due to "insensitive gender-based statements".[2] CBS fired longtime radio show host Don Imus and ESPN pulled fan favorite Colin Cowherd off the air due to racial slurs.[3] Former star Major League Baseball pitcher Curt Schilling was terminated over a social media post that transgenders felt was offensive. Cyber-security firm PacketSled CEO Matt Harrigan was let go shortly after posting on Facebook that he would get a "sniper rifle" and "kill President-elect Donald Trump."[4]

These folks are smart people who were wildly successful in their fields. But they learned the hard way that when insensitivity is involved, there are seldom second chances. Is this right? Probably not, and in my view people have become too easily offended, but be insensitive at your own risk. Learning to express your feelings, concerns, and opinions with tact is a skill worth mastering.

Tales from the Workplace

My good friend, Launie Fleming, Group President over several Senior Aerospace Corporation facilities, shared the following story with me. Launie had booked a dinner with several high-ranking executives of one of his company's largest customers located in the middle of the "Bible belt."

One of the operations in Launie's group had just hired a new VP of marketing named Harry. While Launie had yet to meet Harry, he thought inviting him to the dinner would be a good way to connect with him while allowing Harry to begin to build a relationship with an important customer.

Midway through the evening, Launie became engrossed in a conversation with the executive sitting closest to him, temporarily tuning out the other bantering going on around him. Suddenly, Launie hears Harry telling a series of sexually offensive jokes to the other executives. He tries making eye contact with Harry, shaking his head and frowning in an effort to get Harry to stop. Finally, Launie very forcefully says, "Harry, just stop." But of course, by this time, the damage had already been done.

Later that evening, the customer sends an e-mail to Launie expressing his thorough disgust with the whole affair. The next day, Launie pays an unscheduled visit to Harry's facility, hands him a cardboard box, and tells him to clean out his desk as he is no longer welcome at Senior Aerospace. Harry, due to his insensitivity, has essentially fired himself .[2]

! Indispensable Tip

For goodness sakes, be judicious on what you post on social media such as Twitter, Facebook, Instagram, and Snapchat!

Besides these relatively clear insensitive areas to avoid, there are a few other things leaders often do that can create an impression of social insensitivity. For example, failing to listen and pay full attention to others. If someone comes into your office and says, "got a minute?" either put down your tablet or smartphone and focus on the conversation at hand as if the person in front of you is the most important person in the world, or tell them you are busy and will come see them when you are finished. Realize that in meetings it is exceptionally rude to play with a smartphone or tablet for things unrelated to the subject at hand. If you do use such devices for taking notes, let the meeting leader know that your use of the tablet is related to the meeting.

Another way to show insensitivity is to interrupt others before they have finished their thoughts. Far too many executives abruptly cut people off in mid-sentence like the Meryl Streep character in *The Devil Wears Prada* when she dismissed her associates with a wave of the hand and a curt "That's all."

When meeting someone for the first time, try and find things you are both interested in to talk about. If that is not possible, talk about what *they* enjoy in life. You will not only come off as sensitive to their interests, you will probably become a more well-rounded conversationalist.

Learning how to apologize when you are wrong or insensitive is a great way to show both humility and sensitivity. To paraphrase Gary Chapman and Emily Thomas in their award-winning book, *The Five Languages of Apology*, an effective apology has several important steps. First, we must be sincere. Most of us have pretty powerful "sincerity detectors." In my opinion, cyclist Lance Armstrong's apology on Oprah after he finally admitted to taking performance enhancing drugs failed the sincerity test miserably. In fact, he barely managed to mutter a "sorry" before going on to brag about his skill as a liar.

Next, a good apology requires taking total responsibility. Armstrong not only failed to do this, he basically said he was swept away by a culture of cheating and that he needed to do so to keep the playing field level.

Third, offering some form of restitution is essential. One should say in effect, "What can I do to make this right?" Lance Armstrong not only did not offer any kind of restitution, he actually sued one of his accusers, Emma O'Reilly, for libel and has since tried to fight the US Postal Service for attempting to take back the money the USPS gave the US Cycling Team in a breach of contract lawsuit.[5]

Finally, there should be a promise to try very hard to not make the same mistake again. How many times have you accepted an apology from someone only to see them turn around and make the very same mistake? Remember Congressman Anthony Weiner, the guy who got caught posting lewd photos of himself? Not just on July 23, 2013, but also May 27, 2014, and August 28, 2016. [6] Most of us are forgiving in nature but we do have our limits.

On the flip side, a sincere compliment is a great way to demonstrate awareness, sensitivity, and create a positive vibe with another person. Most of us are constantly bombarded by negativity regarding the things we do or fail to do. I have seen many powerful, wealthy, successful people literally light up when being complimented. How many people do you know that are sick and tired of all the sincere compliments they get?

A Quick Guide to Increasing Social Sensitivity

- Learn to use words like usually, probably, maybe, sometimes, often, or seldom. Try to minimize the use of "you are always" or "you are never."
- Ask people about their interests and converse about those versus talking about your interests.
- Find something that you like about someone you encounter at least once a day then write a note, send an e-mail, or verbally tell them what you admire.
- Let others finish their thoughts before you jump in with yours.
- Practice effective apologies – sincerity – total responsibility – offer restitution – promise not to err again.
- Humor at the expense of others can be very dangerous – stay away from sexual comments, racial slurs, religious conversation, and politics.

Executive Presence

It might be tempting to dismiss the importance of image as a component of your success as a leader, but extensive research over many years has proven that the first impression you make on others can make a dramatic difference on how they evaluate you. Projecting an image to others of how you want them to see you can greatly increase your ability to influence them.

In a June 2014 article in the *Journal of Consumer Research* reviewing numerous studies on image, it was concluded that people respond positively to clothing that matches their expectations – surgeons in scrubs, bankers and lawyers in suits, artists looking trendy, information technology people looking a bit nerdy, etc. In short, we expect a different image from an executive than we do from a rock star. Interestingly, they found one exception. "People whose dress deviates slightly from the norm was seen as positive, suggesting that the individual is powerful enough to risk the social costs of such behaviors."[7] I refer to the image that leaders should try and project as their "executive presence."

John Molloy, in his seminal work, *Dress for Success*, was one of the first to document the critical importance of image to success. In 2014, Dr. Michael W. Kraus, an Assistant Professor of Organization Behavior at Yale University, co-wrote a study for the *Journal of Experimental Psychology*, which showed that clothes that project high social status can increase dominance, confidence, and job performance in competitive environments.

A study published in the August 2015 *Social Psychological and Personality Science Journal* found that wearing formal business attire increased abstract thinking, the ability to craft long-term strategy, and negotiation effectiveness.[8]

Leaders with "executive presence" seem to have a certain magnetism that lasts well beyond the first impression. We tend to admire such people even if we do not know much about them. Because they capture our respect so quickly, people with presence tend to have a huge advantage in establishing rapport.

Dress is just one component of presence. The others are emotional, psychological, and intellectual. The emotional part of presence refers to our mental attitude, how we *feel* about the world.

Are you an optimist or a pessimist? Optimists feel that they have a certain degree of control over their own destiny and that things will somehow work out. Pessimists often feel depressed and focus on all the things that might go wrong and tend to come across as gloomy.

The optimist radiates enthusiasm, which is usually contagious. The pessimist tends to project an anti-change and generally negative attitude. It is not hard to see which behaviors will cause you to be more influential with people.

Another aspect of presence is psychological. The most critical element of the psychological is how we *think* about ourselves. Much of what we think of ourselves is based upon "self-talk." If your thoughts and self-talk are mostly negative, this will eventually be imprinted on your subconscious mind. Do you hear yourself saying things like, "I can't remember names," "I am terrible at sales," or "I cannot seem to catch a break"? If so, you are probably projecting the image of a victim and not that of a leader.

A final aspect of presence is *intellectual*. No, not your IQ. Most of us have plenty of basic intelligence. Presence can be enhanced by accumulating *broad* knowledge. *Deep* knowledge is often the key to success in our given profession. Broad knowledge is what allows us to converse in a meaningful way with a variety of people on a wide range of subjects. Broad knowledge can be useful in bridging social and economic divides. Extensive research has shown that when people feel they have common interests, they have a more favorable view of each other.[9]

Tales from the Workplace

Mark Murphy, CEO and President of the Green Bay Packers (an Aquamarine and fellow Theta Chi Fraternity Brother), exudes executive presence in a mild-mannered way. He told me that he learned a lot about leadership when he played for the Washington Redskins under legendary Coach Joe Gibbs. Mark has based a good portion of his philosophy on many of the same tenets that propelled Coach Gibbs into the NFL Hall of Fame.

Like Coach Gibbs, Mark endeavors to make himself accessible to anyone in the organization who needs him. He stops by people's offices just to check in and see how they are doing.

This allows him to take the pulse of the organization in a less formal way.

Mark believes that his main job is to be supportive of his people by giving them what they need to successfully do their jobs. After all he says, "I hired them for expertise that I do not have. Also I think it is a mistake to fire people too quickly. Every executive, coach, player, and team goes through rough patches. If you have been diligent in the hiring process, they should be given the chance to turn things around."

Mark is a student of management and is a big proponent of strategic planning and yearly goal setting. In his view, "It serves as a guide that can keep me from making decisions out of expediency or the emotion of the moment." Once people clearly know what is expected of them, we engage in regular communication as to how they are doing so there are no surprises at the yearend evaluation.

When it comes to dress, Mark claims to be old school, almost always dressing in a suit. He says that dressing as an executive serves to remind him that he represents one of the premier franchises in professional sports and as such, should show as much class as he can.

Mark smiles often and tries to force himself to project energy even when he is exhausted. He has found that smiles beget smiles in return, and others naturally become inspired to be more energetic themselves. Mark says that he is constantly on the lookout for the things his people are doing well and then he tries to be effusive in his praise in front of others. He claims that he has yet to meet a person who does not respond positively to sincere thanks and appreciation.

A Quick Guide to Increasing Executive Presence

- Be open with people; it can be very disarming.
- Enunciate your words.
- Learn to make your verbal communication crisp.

- Dress a half level more formally than others. If your people dress in jeans and T-shirts, wear slacks and a blouse or polo shirt. If your people wear slacks and polos, wear a blazer or jacket. If your people wear blazers, dress more formally in a suit.
- Learn to project your voice in a conference room or meeting.
- Look people in the eye.
- Walk tall with a spring in your step.
- Eliminate negative "self-talk."
- Train yourself to see the possibilities in situations, not just the negatives.
- Accumulate broad knowledge on a variety of types like sports, current events, music, the visual arts, etc.

Flexibility

In today's dynamic world, leaders need to develop the ability to adapt quickly to changing circumstances. I have followed dozens of leaders around during their workdays and almost universally, they seem to have every minute of the day scheduled with meetings, events, e-mails, etc. Yet on average, at least a third of the things that leaders have to deal with pop up unexpectedly – the crisis that erupts, the drop-in visitor who needs something immediately, or the e-mail bomb that explodes from a customer, supplier, or other constituent. So, if the day is already completely scheduled, how does a leader deal with the things that are difficult to plan for?

The answer, short of working extremely long hours or on weekends, is twofold. First you must leave at least a couple hours unscheduled to handle these unexpected interruptions. Even if you are on electronic scheduling, put in a few "phantom" meetings so you can have time to catch up. Second you must learn to say "no" in a nice way to unreasonable requests for your time or attendance in meetings.

Of course, we all want to be the "go-to" person, but this does not mean acquiescing to every demand someone wants to burden you with. It is okay to let your boss know what things will drop off if you take on an assignment. It is also acceptable to ask for more time on occasion or more resources if the situation warrants it. After all, most high-level leaders did not get there by being irrational. Often times they simply do not know how long things will take unless it is pointed out to them. Get in the habit of thinking up creative alternatives and suggesting them to the boss. Be careful not to act like a victim or complainer. Every organization has time, budget, equipment, and personnel limitations. If these constraints are reasonable, we need to do the best we can to perform well within those limitations.

Part of flexibility also comes from learning to interact with powerful, sophisticated, or unsophisticated people equally well. I was born and raised in a lower-middle-class family and honestly did not know powerful or sophisticated people back then. Over the years, as I started to deal with more sophisticated people as the norm, I developed a level of comfort in that arena, but it was initially stressful. These days, my struggle is to remember my roots and deal with the less sophisticated folks I encounter in a more productive manner. The world is composed of wealthy, powerful, famous, highly educated, sophisticated, uneducated, and unsophisticated people. Great leaders adapt and create comfort with everyone they come in contact with.

Tales from the World of Entertainment

Shawn Imitates-Dog is a power player in the whirling dervish world of live sports and entertainment. In addition to his current role of Vice President, Human Resources at Live Nation, he has worked for Creative Arts Agency and the sports powerhouse AEG Worldwide. Shawn explained to me that the two keys to success in the entertainment world are relationships and flexibility. In Shawn's experience, Hollywood is made up of an intricate web of connections. "Let's have lunch" is not just pleasantry, it is an expectation. He spends the better part of his workday creating and cultivating mutually supportive relationships both internally and externally.

At Live Nation, he meets with each member of the executive team at least twice per week – often with a specific agenda in mind and sometimes just to talk. Shawn believes that it would be impossible to have the bonds of respect and trust with his peers without a heavy investment of time spent together.

Unlike many in the human resources community, Shawn sees himself as an entertainment executive who specializes in human resources versus an HR person who just happens to work in entertainment. The distinction in the entertainment world is critical. Things move at light speed in his industry and folks who focus solely on the legalistic or compliance aspects of the job wash out. As a true partner, Shawn's view is that HR should be 80 percent support and 20 percent compliance. Because of the relationship's he has built with his peers, he can get them to see both sides of issues when he has to revert to compliance mode.

Externally, Shawn has developed into something of a legend relationship-wise. His list of contacts is both long and distinguished. He takes as a point of pride acknowledging everyone in his network who contacts him. He responds quickly via text, e-mail, phone call, or personal visits depending upon the need.

In terms of flexibility, Shawn's experience has proved that the number one reason leaders fail in the entertainment world is due to their inability to adapt to the constantly changing landscape in the industry. "In food service, taste buds change and people are always looking for the 'new' restaurant theme. In music, there is always a need for the fresh act or even a new genre. In sports, teams unexpectedly make it into the playoffs requiring quick changes in venue setup, ticket sales, personnel rapid re-deployment, and the like. All our businesses succeed due to creativity and we have found that too much emphasis on structure kills the creative spirit. And because we like to run lean, when there are job openings, they must be filled quickly, as every unfilled position is costing us money.

"So, the things we look for personality-wise in our leaders are the ability to change direction on a dime without getting stressed out, the humility to do any task necessary to get the show up and running no matter how menial, and leaders who are willing to take the time to build relationships."

In the world of "shock TV," we are led to believe that the world is "either,or" where no middle ground can be found. Either you are Democrat, Republican, Green Party, or Libertarian. In religion, it is Christian, Muslim, Buddhist, Jewish, or Atheist. Pro-life or Pro-choice. Globalist or Isolationist. Traditional man and woman marriage or same-sex marriage. The business world is comprised of all of the above and then some. The truly adaptable leader must respect the views and values of everyone even though it may go against the grain of our own beliefs. So *tolerance* is required at the minimum.

A Quick Guide to Becoming More Flexible

- Every work day, unplanned events occur. Do not jam your schedule so full that you have no room to maneuver.
- Learn to at least tolerate and perhaps even appreciate the differences in others. You do not have to embrace their viewpoint or lifestyle but your life will be fuller and you will be much more productive if you are not so narrow minded.
- Put yourself in positions where you interact with people of different organizational levels and socio-economic strata. You will find that powerful, rich, educated, or sophisticated people all have flaws and are therefore much like you. You will find the less educated or unsophisticated people often have great talents in some areas. All people have flaws and value.

Confident Body Language

Let's say you have received a complaint that one of your direct reports is sexually harassing one of his associates. When you see him while walking the halls, you casually mention to him that when he has a minute, you would like to talk with him in your office. He has no idea that you have received a complaint. Later, as the employee enters your office, you smile and ask him to take a seat. You open the conversation with some chit chat. You notice that the employee appears open, relaxed, looks intently at you, and leans back in his chair.

As you get into the matter of the sexual harassment complaint, the employee starts to change. Suddenly arms are crossed, his body seems rigid, there is limited eye contact, and his hands are tightly gripping the armrests of the seat. As he tries to explain his view of the situation, he resists looking you in the eye, squirms in his seat, and his throat starts to tighten. You finish the meeting by telling him that you will be objective when investigating the complaint.

Even though his story may have sounded just as plausible as the complaint, you really do not believe much of what he said because his body language gave you the impression that he was hiding something. In essence, body movements, gestures, voice tone, and facial expressions were communicating far more clearly than the spoken word.

Body language communicates instantaneously. When someone "flips you the bird," not much else is required to understand how the person feels. Pointing at someone, shrugging shoulders, and smacking the side of your head when you were careless or forgot something seem to universally communicate the same things to people of many different cultures. There are six areas of body language that leaders should be aware of in the signals they are sending – eyes, face, arms, posture, hands, and gait.

Eyes

Perhaps the eyes are the best indicators of a person's inner feelings. Psychologists have long concluded that trustworthy people tend to look people straight in the eyes while dishonest folks usually avoid eye contact when they are caught in a lie. People with low self-esteem also tend to avert eye contact.

By watching someone's eye gestures, it is very easy to correctly gauge their thoughts. Raising an eyebrow shows that you are skeptical, while raising two is an indication of being surprised. A smile and nod signal agreement, whereas eyes looking up into their head often mean they are seriously thinking about what you said and are trying to process it.

Face

Next to eyes, a person's facial expressions are the second-best indicator of their feelings. Clinched jaws indicate anger, a sneer means contempt, frowns demonstrate unhappiness, while smiles show joy.

Arms

Open arms usually indicate comfort or acceptance. Crossed arms signal defensiveness or discomfort. They seemingly serve as a barrier against an impending attack.

Posture

Sitting on the edge of a chair usually means the person is engaged. Sitting back in a chair with an arm draped over a table indicates the person is relaxed. Sitting with the back of the chair facing forward straddling the seat often communicates an attitude of superiority.

Hands

Wringing hands generally mean a person is worried; clenched fists often show anger. Standing with hands behind one's back shows authority. Clasping both hands behind the head and leaning back shows confidence. Stroking the chin or a finger on the lips can communicate that you are thinking. Boredom is conveyed by putting an elbow on the table, opening the palm of one hand, and sinking the chin into the open palm.

Gait

People who walk fast tend to be on a mission. People who glide demonstrate confidence. Depressed people shuffle along, head down, hands in their pockets. Deep thinkers tend to walk head down, hands clasped behind their backs.[10]

Be advised, however, that body language is not always 100% accurate as to what is being communicated. If your wife wears flannel pajamas to bed, it probably means she's not in the mood for sex. Then again, it could simply mean that she feels cold!

A Quick Guide to Confident Body Language

- Walk either swiftly or symphonically
- Maintain eye contact with the person you are speaking with, but occasionally break contact. It is not a staring contest.
- Smile and nod when you agree with something the other person has said.
- Try to avoid crossing your arms around other people. It will be harder for them to relate to you and it sometimes shows a lack of confidence.
- When sitting, either sit forward on the edge of your chair or sit back relaxed, depending upon what message you are trying to send.
- Pay close attention to the signals your hands are sending. Try not to let your hands indicate boredom, anger, or worry.

Effective Conflict Handling

Conflict is a disagreement between two or more individuals, teams, or organizations who feel they have incompatible goals. Conflicts arise when something one party does is seen as interfering with the needs or objectives of the other party. Conflicts typically occur when there are conflicting goals, philosophical differences, scarce resources, or a difference in the interpretation of events or behaviors. If a relationship lasts long enough, there will be disagreements of one kind or another. Unless these conflicts can be resolved effectively, the relationship is unlikely to endure. Poorly handled conflicts result in hostility, stonewalling, and damaged relationships. But when successfully dealt with, conflicts can result in novel approaches, needed change, or even more satisfying relationships. Without conflict, there is often stagnation and apathy.

There are three main causes of conflict – personal style differences, communication issues, and resource scarcity.

Personal Style Differences

In Chapter 2, we saw that the six interpersonal styles have very different views on how the world should be and how people should act. We tend to get along with people who see things the way we see them and have trouble with people who hold opposing views. Prejudice, ignorance, education, upbringing, generation differences, and experience levels are other factors that create conflict on a personal level.

Communication Difficulties

Sometimes poor communication is simply a matter of semantics. People may be thinking along the same lines, but the words they choose have different meanings to the other person than was intended. Ineffective listening can also be the culprit. We tend to hear the things that support our views while ignoring the rest. Some people are so thin skinned that they take offense at the pettiest perceived slight. Frequently it is unclear who has responsibility for what tasks because the leader has simply failed to clearly communicate to the affected parties.

Resource Scarcity

If time, money, and equipment were unlimited and everyone could play the role they wanted to play, the overwhelming amount of conflicts in organizations would simply disappear. Disagreements over goals, priorities, performance criteria, budgets, schedules, promotions, compensation, head count, office space, and the like are common occurrences in most organizations. So determining the root cause of the conflict is essential to deciding how the situation should be handled. Kenneth W. Thomas laid out five conflict handling strategies that have served as the basis for most conflict management approaches. They are: *competing, accommodating, compromising, collaborating, and avoiding.* Each of these strategies has certain strengths and limitations. The key is learning when and how to use each of the five. However, it has been my experience that most people only use, on average, three of the five styles, almost totally ignoring the benefits of the other two.

Competing

Competing is when you attempt to achieve your goals while giving as little as possible to the other party. Examples would be fighting hard in a meeting to get your way or using formal authority to stifle dissent. Competing works best when you are absolutely right and the other person is dead wrong and it is important that the right decision be made. Competing also makes sense when the commitment of the other party to implement the solution is not that important.

The problem with competing too often is that "losers" spend a lot of energy trying to win the next time around and you end up creating enemies for the future. You may also end up winning the battle at the expense of the long-term relationship.

Accommodating

This strategy is the opposite of competing. Essentially, you give in to the demands or needs of the other person and do not fight very hard to get much of anything in return. Accommodating works best when something is much more important to the other party than it is to you or to preserve a longer-term relationship. It obviously is the smart thing to do when the other person turns out to be right and you realize that you are wrong. You can also use this strategy to build up a bank account of goodwill with the other party that can be drawn upon in the future.

The problem with too frequent accommodation is that you may be perceived as a "soft touch" and will be counted upon to "cave in" most of the time. People who constantly give in end up frustrated, unhappy, and disillusioned, all of which may harden into resentment of the other person.

Compromising

In compromising, the idea is to be moderately assertive in getting what you want while being moderately cooperative in giving the other side some of what they want. Both parties essentially realize that they can only get a part of what they desire. This strategy makes sense when half of what you want will solve the problem or when the two parties are of roughly equal power and it is the best deal you can get. It is a poor strategy when half a solution is only marginally better than no solution. Too frequent compromise potentially locks you out of better deals that might be had if both parties took the time to look for creative "out of the box" solutions.

Collaborating

The term win-win solution is thrown around way too often these days. The true definition of collaboration is when both parties take the time to try and get most, if not all, of what they want out of a conflict situation. True collaboration requires open dialogue, listening to understand differences between the parties, creativity in coming up with potentially ground-breaking options, and careful deliberation over these options to make a decision that is beneficial to all. Collaboration works best when there is little time pressure, and when the issue is too important to both sides to compromise. If time is not pressing, it's a great place to start because one can always fall back to competing, accommodating, compromising, or simply walk away.

Avoiding

My first boss when I was a supervisor at International Paper used to drive me crazy with a line he uttered seemingly every other day, "John, my decision is to not make a decision at this time." For the life of me, I could not understand how failure to make decisions was ever a good thing to do. Years later, I now realize that not every conflict requires assertive action. On occasion, withdrawing from or postponing a decision is the best option. Avoidance works best when you are in the heat of anger, the facts needed to make a good choice are not yet available, or the problem is likely to resolve itself with no action taken. The downside of this strategy is that most issues do not resolve themselves, and after extended avoidance, the time pressure to act is greater and the options left tend to be fewer.

> **!**
>
> ## Essential Knowledge About the Person You are Having a Conflict With
>
> - What is important to them?
> - What kind of time pressure are they under?
> - Who has the upper hand power-wise?
> - What can you use as leverage?

Three Things to do when the Conflict Becomes Emotional

Always Be Respectful

During emotional conflicts, it is easy to become disrespectful yourself. Carelessly chosen words can cause wounds that are difficult to heal. Regardless of how angry or abrasive the other person may get, it is imperative that you keep your head about you and not fall into a tit-for-tat exchange. It helps to keep your end goals in mind, one of which should always be to try and maintain a relationship with the person after the conflict subsides.

Try and See Their Position

You will have a much better chance at getting what you want if you can put yourself in the other person's shoes and understand their feelings and point of view. Your goal is to understand, not necessarily agree with their positions. Make sure that you let them know that you understand where they are coming from by restating your understanding of what they have said.

Share Your Position and Feelings

When in conflict with someone, it is usually better to present your case in as brief a manner as you can. Stay away from words that might inflame the situation. In short, what is your view? What do you need? And, how are you feeling?

A Quick Guide to Conflict Handling Styles

Competing

- Works best when issues are important to you, when you are definitely right, when time is critical, and when others lack the expertise that you have.
- Causes problems when you value a long-term relationship, when issues are complex, and when in conflict with powerful or successful people.

Accommodating

- Works best when the issue is more important to them than to you, when you lack their expertise, when you are wrong, or when you want to preserve a long-term relationship.
- Causes problems when others are wrong or are likely to take advantage of your good nature in the future.

Compromising

- Works best when it is unlikely you will be able to get everything you want, when half a solution will solve the problem, or when the other person has power equal to yours.
- Causes problems when half a solution does not really solve the problem or when long-term solutions are needed.

Collaborating

- Works best when the commitment of others is needed and where there are potential solutions that can give both parties everything they need.
- Causes problems when time is critical or when the other party is not interested in seeing you get much of anything.

Avoiding

- Works best when emotions are too high to think rationally, when the data needed to make a good resolution is not available, or when no action may solve the problem.
- Causes problems when issues are unlikely to solve themselves and you are responsible for solving the conflict.

CHAPTER 4

STRATEGY 3 – GENERATE THE POWER
OF THE PYRAMID

"You can be strong, you can be authoritative, but you can
also be nice and make people want to deal with you."

Nancy Kanter, EVP, Original Programming,
Disney Junior Worldwide

AN IMPORTANT REASON to become more interpersonally
effective is to increase your ability to influence the organization's
associates to alter the way things are done in an effort to further the
aims of the enterprise. Creating an effective power base to make this
happen is essential. All leaders have numerous potential means of
influence at their disposal. Understanding the advantages and disad-
vantages of these various bases of power and picking the right one(s)
to use in any given situation is an extremely important consideration.

Building Your Power Base

Visualize a pyramid that is wide at the base and gets progressively
smaller at the top, as shown in Diagram A. It has been my experience that leaders too often start out attempting to use the bases of
influence from the top down, which is precisely the *wrong* way to
go about it.

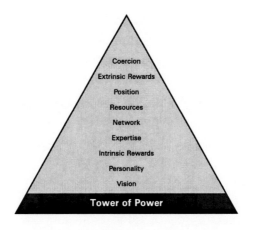

Diagram A

Avoiding Coercion

The top four sections of the pyramid can be thought of as "push" forms of influence. People feel pushed into doing what the leader wants done. At the very top is *coercion*. This refers to negative consequences such as expulsion, isolation, public humiliation, withholding resources, or anything that a person might feel threatened by. There are many problems inherent in the use of this type of power. First, it is very fragile. The organization gives a leader the ability to coerce people but can instantly take it away. Second, it mostly works when the leader is physically present. We all remember the iron-fisted teacher who, when out of the room or when a "substitute" was teaching, saw all the discipline go out the window. Third, coercion causes people to do the bare minimum necessary to stop the pain and typically not one thing more. Lastly, people who feel coerced tend to spend a lot of energy trying to figure out how to avoid the pressure or worse, coerce back.

> ## ! Indispensable Tip
> Coercion should *never* be used as the first option. It should *always* be held in reserve until other possibilities are explored.

In today's world, our associates often have more coercive power over us than we would like to admit. They could for instance, hire a contingency fee attorney with no money out-of-pocket to threaten us with litigation, knowing that many organizations will settle out of court. If a lawsuit goes to trial, we end up spending countless hours in depositions, fulfilling document requests, lining up witnesses, and the like. Or they could go to the local news media and allege anything. The story will make page one of the business section and create a public relations nightmare. If we spend the time to investigate the claims and prepare a response, it will be buried in the back pages of the paper.

Coerced associates could choose to sabotage key organization systems. In the information technology world, one string of code tapped in by a disgruntled employee could crash the whole kit-and-caboodle.

If our enterprise is a government contractor or of sufficient size, an associate could file a complaint with a whole host of agencies such as the equal employment opportunity commission, internal revenue service, or comptroller. If you want a real paper chase, just try proving to a watchdog agency that you *didn't* do something.

I'm not saying coercive power is not good to have or that a leader should never use it. Rather, it should be a last resort and not a leader's first option. Yet sadly, even in today's supposedly more progressive business world, far too many people in positions of authority use fear and intimidation tactics all too frequently. The goal of influence in the workplace is to ensure you have not jeopardized your ability to influence these same people again in the future. With coercion, you can expect just the opposite.

Limiting Extrinsic Rewards

One level down the pyramid is *extrinsic rewards* or, in a sense, bribery. In the use of this type of influence, a leader engages in a sort of quid pro quo with associates. Essentially the idea is to hold out "carrots" such as pay raises, promotions, desirable task force assignments, favorable geographic locations, or other "perks" in exchange for moving in a desired direction.

This base of influence is also very fragile, in that the organization can easily take these "carrots" away. At some point, a leader literally runs out of things that can be given to associates. I mean really, what more can high-tech companies such as Google or SAS Software give their people than they already provide? And as several military officers have told me over the years, "The thing which causes a soldier to jump on a hand grenade to save a buddy is not combat pay or the thought of a medal awarded posthumously."

Don't Forget This

Extrinsic rewards tend to motivate for a very short period of time and form a higher floor of expectations for the future. And perhaps worst of all, you end up with a mercenary workforce. Once another organization tops what you provide, those are the people you lose.

Once again, it is nice to have these types of things as bargaining chips, but it should be further down the list.

Don't Rely on Your Position

The next stage of the pyramid is *position power*. This refers to the legitimacy of being called CEO, president, senior executive vice president, and the like. It also is tied to one's authority to back, approve, or support the proposals of associates.

Frankly, after the scandals of inflated body counts in Vietnam, phantom weapons of mass destruction in Iraq, citizen abuses by police officers in Ferguson, Missouri, Charlotte, North Carolina, and Baltimore, Maryland, the defrocking of religious leaders Jim Bakker, Ted Haggard, and Jimmy Swaggart, and the Enron, Worldcom, Adelphia, and Tyco fiascos, formal position power doesn't come close to having the impact it once had. Just try telling your teenage son or daughter, "Do it because I'm your father and I'm telling you to do it." This never worked well with my son, and I trust it won't work well with yours either. Public opinion polls in recent years consistently show that the majority of employees do not trust the public pronouncements of their senior-most executives.

> ### Don't Forget This
> Trying to appeal to Generation X and Millennial associates with formal authority is pointless.

This base of power is also very fragile in that the organization gives you the legitimacy of authority and can instantly take it away. Consider what happens to US presidents and their staffs on Inauguration Day. At the beginning of the day the outgoing president is the most powerful person in the world and hours later is just an ordinary citizen. In his book, *Crisis*, Hamilton Jordan, President Carter's Chief of Staff, reveals that in the hours leading up to the swearing in of President Reagan, he and his staff were making final arrangements for the release of the American hostages from Iran. There was considerable uncertainty as to the timing of the expected release. Moments after President Reagan was sworn in, Jordan tried to call his assistant to check on the status of the hostages. After a brief pause, she came back on the line and said simply, "Mr. Jordan, you are no longer cleared for that information." It was at that moment Jordan realized how much of his power had been tied to his position and how quickly it was taken away.[1]

Like the other bases of power outlined so far, having formal authority is great and often helpful, but it should not be relied upon too heavily.

Don't Waste Resources

The last of the "push" forms of influence is *resource power*. This is a less personal form of bribery and includes providing budget, materials, space, time, staff support, data, and the like. Individuals who can provide the most critical and difficult to obtain resources come to have significant power. Think of supply sergeants in the Army or budget directors in the government. However, this form of influence has exactly the same limitations as the other form of extrinsic rewards outlined earlier.

In an ideal scenario, a leader might be able to throw massive amounts of money, people, or other resources at a challenge. A New York Yankees approach if you will. But under the more severe resource constraints most organizations are faced with, this option is a non-starter. Most leaders are forced to seek solutions where they optimize the resources they can amass around some strategic theme. This requires hard choices to be made.

The Push and Pull of Networking

In the middle of the pyramid is *Network*. This form of influence can be used to "push" or "pull." Basically, networking refers to using your relations with influential people to either threaten or help others.

In the threatening use of a network, I liken it to "murder for hire." In my consulting practice, I never have any formal position inside of the organizations I work with. I couldn't *personally* fire, demote, or cause anyone inside the organization to be isolated. But if I could convince people that I have a better relationship with an internal power broker that could do those things than they have, then I have de facto ability to coerce from a distance.

Tales from the Workplace

Let me provide an example of the "pull" use of a network. I was conducting a strategic planning session with one of my clients a few years ago. A competitor had just come out with an innovation that made one of my client's products obsolete overnight. This item represented roughly 30 percent of the organization's revenue. They felt there was no way to respond since it was December and the industry trade shows, where all of the buying decisions took place, were scheduled to be held less than a month away. Historically in this company, it took nine months to create a prototype, get samples made, and produce initial shipment quantities, since all their engineering and manufacturing were done in-house. They were all set to abdicate 30 percent of their revenue base to their competitor.

In pushing the team further, it became apparent that all they really needed were prototypes and spec sheets to take to the shows. The product didn't even need to work just yet; it merely had to look like the finished product would look. Fortunately they had already engaged a patent attorney to provide counsel on the specifications and appearance the product would need to avoid violating their competitor's patent.

I was able to introduce them to two people in my network who were able to do 48-hour turnaround on computer aided design prototypes and two others who could produce in China the initial several thousand units needed within 90 days to stock their dealers' shelves. In the end, they were able to keep their market share and prevent the competitor from making further inroads. While I *personally* had no idea how to make quick prototypes or any experience with manufacturing in China, people in my network did. How much influence do you think that buys me with this client in the future?

If you do not have much of a network, start by building one inside your organization. Then use LinkedIn to add external business contacts. LinkedIn is the modern equivalent of previous generations having to join the country club, bowling league, or service groups like the Elks Club or Lion's Club in order to develop a network. Personally, I spend on average seven hours a week adding to or cultivating my leadership network. I consider it some of the most important time I invest in my business.

Mark Burnett, the father of reality TV (*Survivor*, *The Apprentice*, *Dancing with the Stars*, *The Bachelor*), is not afraid to tap into his vast network when searching for ideas or solving problems. He says, "The bottom line is that only results count. How you arrive at them does not. Few people know that the only show that was my original idea was *Survivor*. Yet I get the credit for all the other programs that followed."[2]

Pull Forms of Influence

Expertise

The first of the four "pull" forms of influence is *expertise*. This is a leader's credentials, degrees, certifications, technical prowess, and track record of success. A nice thing about this base of power is that it is not fragile. Once a leader possesses these things, no one can take them away. Most people are much more likely to follow someone who has some kind of proof that they should know what they are talking about.[3]

I once interviewed a famous Hollywood movie director who has won several Academy Awards. He told me that unless someone is a well-known actor or actress, the only thing that counts in the movie business is a person's track record. Because the film industry is a relatively small community, one bad performance and one may never work again. And the truth is, most businesses or professions are also small worlds where most of the players and their reputations are well known.

Indispensable Tip

Your reputation is your "personal brand." Guard it jealously and always be on the lookout for ways to enhance it through lifelong learning and piling up your credentials.

The thing experts have to guard against is over-complicating their communication with non-experts. Research indicates that once we learn something, it is difficult for us to imagine not knowing it. Thus, experts tend to either omit key contextual data or talk as if everyone understands at the same level they do.

Tales from the Workplace

The Chief Human Resources Officer (CHRO) leading the strategic planning effort for a $900 million global electronics company is not something you see very often. Then again, that is because very few companies have a leader like Hedley Lawson in the top HR role.

In his long and distinguished career, Hedley has held the top HR slot in several large companies and is currently the managing partner at Aligned Growth Partners, LLC in the San Francisco Bay Area. He has always been an equal with his peers in influencing the direction of the organization because he took it upon himself to learn to speak their language. While others in his field were chasing HR certifications Hedley was boning up on strategy, finance, operations, marketing, international business, cultures, and sales.

Hedley strongly believes that using expertise as a basis for building relationships is one of the most powerful ways to exert influence. Yet especially in his field of Human Resources, he sees very few leaders even see the need, let alone take the time to build this power base. "Oh sure" he says, "HR has certifications galore <u>within</u> the field." But as he sees it this has caused the profession to be inward focused and out of touch with the business itself.

Hedley has some powerful statistics to back this up. Fewer than half the respondents in a recent National Association of Corporate Directors survey rated HR's value to the board as good or great in 8 of 11 areas. The CHRO role was rated lower than any other c-suite role other than the Chief Marketing Officer in terms of how much their influence has grown in the last five years. And only 19% of CHROs are even invited to board meetings versus 91% for Chief Financial Officers. Even if the CHRO is fortunate enough to get a seat at the big table, it seems they have precious little influence.

Hedley believes that forging personal relationships is great (and I know he is very good at it). But the most effective way to

> relate to top-level leaders in other disciplines is to have something in common to talk about. And that common language should be planning, strategy, finance, operations, and the like.

Intrinsic Rewards

The next "pull" form of influence is *intrinsic* rewards. Ask a thousand people – and I have – the question, "Think of a time when you couldn't wait to get to work. A time when you woke up at 1 a.m. tossing and turning with ideas in your head. You took out a pad of paper, jotted down notes, and tried to go back to sleep. You continued to toss and turn and seemed filled with adrenaline. Finally, at 4:30 a.m., you gave up on getting sleep, got dressed, and drove to work in the dark. You skipped lunch and dinner, and looked at the clock amazed that it was 6:30 p.m. What was going on that caused you to be so excited?"

By the way, if you have never had such an experience, it is very sad, because you probably have never truly been "in the zone." Natural chemicals called endorphins, encephalons, and oxytocins are released in the brain during such peak events. They can be just as addictive as manufactured pain blockers or stimulants. Once you have experienced them, it is hard to live any other way.

The answers that kept coming up time and time again were *challenge, achievement, recognition, freedom, and growth.* These are as close to universal motivators as you will find. We all differ on the level of challenge, the type of recognition and the kind of growth that will be motivating, but these are the things that cause great effort to be expended in pursuit of a goal.

Tales from the Workplace

To demonstrate the power of becoming a leader that can tap into and fulfill people's intrinsic needs, consider this. One of my clients, an aerospace company, hired the first outsider to run a major division of its organization. The outsider had left his position as president of a smaller company in Southern California and asked three of his key lieutenants to join him in the new venture. He offered them the same title, similar pay, same type of industry, and they had to uproot their families and move to the Rocky Mountains. Each agreed to do so. When I asked why they chose to take what was essentially a lateral move, each person said they had never worked for a better boss. When I probed further as to what made him so great, each of the three said something to the effect of, "He puts me in very challenging situations, gives me a reasonable resource allocation to allow me a fighting chance of success, rewards me when I do well, coaches me when I struggle, allows me the autonomy to do things in the manner I think is best, and keeps me on the steep part of the learning curve so I never get bored." Now that's a boss to emulate!

Well it turns out that this fellow was a "turnaround" manager who normally likes to keep moving around. Sure enough, three years later he left the company to take a job as a division president in the Pacific Northwest. The same three people once again quit their jobs and uprooted their families a second time for the same reason. Within three years, the leader quit again to take the presidency of an organization back in Southern California. And you guessed it, the same three people followed him back to the place it all started, this time unable to even afford the quality of house they sold six years earlier because of the rapid appreciation of Southern California real estate. He had become a truly addictive boss by never losing sight of the universal motivators.

Personality Power

Nearing the bottom of the pyramid is *personality*. Included in this base of influence would be things like approachability, likability, genuine flattery, authenticity, constructive criticism, personal warmth, and having the other person's best interests in mind.

Think about it: What wouldn't you do for your best friend? Yet, unless you work for your best friend, can that person give you a raise? Promote you? Assign you a bigger or better office? Let you run a prestigious task force? Give you more time on tasks or a higher budget allocation? Generally not.

But I would be willing to bet that if your best friend called you at 2 a.m. from the jailhouse asking you to bail him out, you would immediately spring into action, no questions asked. Why? Because that person fills a need all people feel – to be tightly connected with someone else Our best friends treat us with respect. They praise us when we need a "pick-me-up." When they criticize us, we know deep down that they are truly trying to help us. Personality power is also about humility or lack of ego.

Human nature being what it is, we tend to be far more influenced by people we like than those we don't. When we mirror the behavior, speech, or appearance of another person, we are creating rapport. People who are like one another tend to like one another. And people who do things that allow others to feel good about themselves tend to be seen as magnetically attractive.

Two-time NBA MVP Stephen Curry has a surprising lack of ego for a superstar. People who know him well say they have never seen someone so successful be so humble. The Spaceship Company President Enrico Palermo flies commercial, does not have his own parking space, and has his desk on the factory floor so everyone has easy access to him. The "commoner's touch" gives him extraordinary influence with people. Ford CEO Alan Mulally put his ego aside and had the courage to say that he largely accelerated a plan for turning around the company that was created by someone else, acknowledged what he didn't know about the car business, and empowered those on his staff who did.[4]

In my opinion, quite a bit of the appeal of Ronald Reagan and Barack Obama can be traced to their personalities. Both made frequent use of self-deprecating humor, smiled often, tried to talk about areas of mutual interest when in conversation with others, and endeavored to end interactions with sincere compliments. Charm is seductive, and everyone is prone to seduction. The importance of personality as a powerful base of influence should not be underestimated.

Tales from the Workplace

Kim Chiodi, Senior Vice President, Human Resources at Western Southern Financial in Cincinnati is easily in the top one percent in her profession. People who work for her say she is compassionate, driven, bright, sophisticated, and has an amazing amount of knowledge about all the HR related areas.

After working for several years at Western Southern, Kim left to start her own consulting practice. Executives of Kim's talent and dedication are difficult to find, so CEO John F. Barrett would periodically attempt to lure her back to the company. Each time, Kim would politely decline saying that she was very happy with her life and consulting career.

Kim was a board member of the Montessori School that her seven-year-old son was attending. Each year the school holds an Oratory Festival where the students in each grade are required to develop and deliver a speech in front of the rest of the class. The school had a tradition of inviting business and community leaders to give a speech to the class to show them how speeches should be delivered. Knowing that Kim had numerous contacts, the board president asked her if she could line up a speaker.

A leader Kim had the utmost respect for was her old boss, John Barrett. She describes John as the most humble, talented, caring, and visionary leader she has ever worked for. As an example of his leadership style, Kim said that he makes it a habit to walk around the cafeteria eating ice cream and engaging anyone at any level who might be there at the time. He has regular breakfast meetings with associates who recently joined Western Southern. During these breakfasts, John regales them with stories of his 28-year career at the company, shares his vision, and attempts to answer all their questions.

Kim explained that John takes the long view of leading a company. He bemoans the fact that because the average tenure of a CEO in American business is around four years that they tend to make self-serving more expedient decisions without regard for long-haul impact. John by contrast wants Western Southern to be a legendary company well after he is gone.

The Montessori School Board President was blown away when Kim announced that it would be John F. Barrett, the CEO of an organization with <u>$66 billion</u> of assets under management who would be addressing the second graders at Montessori. Now picture this, the CEO arrives decked out in his finest suit, walks into the room, and sees all the kids sitting on the floor in a circle with Kim's son proudly standing at attention to greet and introduce <u>his</u> guest. Kim reports that John gave the same polished professional speech delivered with his own brand of passion that he would have given had the audience been made up of the most powerful leaders in Cincinnati. And he stuck around long enough to answer all their questions! That is about all you need to know to see why John Barrett is adored in his company. That is a leader who uses personality to win people over.

The upshot of the story ends with John saying to Kim, "It is time for you to come back home to Western Southern." Kim, teary eyed, accepts John's offer this time telling me, "How could I not want to work for someone like that who did something that made my son feel so special?" And as they say, the rest is history.

Vision

Forming the base of the pyramid is *vision*, or essentially "winning hearts and minds." James MacGregor Burns in his seminal work, *Leadership*, referred to this as Transformational Leadership.[5]

Sometimes a person will be expressive and able to light up a stage like Donald Trump, but this part of vision is the least important. Think about the consumer advocate Ralph Nader, billionaire Warren Buffet, or Mitt Romney. For over five decades, millions of people have been drawn to the consumer movement Nader started; millions more hang on every word of Buffett, and Mitt Romney became a nominee of the Republican Party for President of the United States. Yet they are three of the least dynamic people you will ever come across.

So, why do people follow visionary leaders, even those who are not personally electrifying? Generally, these leaders tap into some of our most basic needs, including the desire for *direction* and the need to find *meaning*.

Transformational leaders have a clear orienting vision. Passion for the cause. A moral conviction that their cause is just. They hold themselves to very high expectations and serve as role models themselves that others seek to emulate.

Cult leaders, though in the darkest of ways, are the epitome of visionary leaders. The ability of Jim Jones and the People's Temple, David Koresh and the Branch Davidians, Warren Jeffs and the Utah polygamist cult, and Marshall Applewhite and Heaven's Gate to get dozens of people to kill themselves "en masse" or otherwise demean themselves shows the incredible power of direction and meaning, even if it is in pursuit of insanity.

One of the movies that I have my coaching clients watch is *The Last Castle*. This story depicts a highly decorated Marine Corps General Officer, played by Robert Redford, who is imprisoned as a result of an error in judgment, attempting to overthrow the brutal prison warden played by James Gandolfini. The warden has all the "push" forms of power on his side and doesn't hesitate to use them. But the Redford character knows that the true battle will be won by capturing the hearts and minds of not only the other inmates, but also the prison guards. He creates a compelling vision of who they can be versus how the rest of the world may view them. In the end, despite having all the "push" forms of power at his disposal, the warden is removed from command. Even though the movie is fictional, there are powerful lessons to be learned.

Tales from the Workplace

Teresa Schlegel, Vice President, Human Resources for Packsize International in Salt Lake City has been my good friend and colleague for 31 years. Her success as a leader in such renowned companies as Orbital ATK, Wilson Sporting Goods, and Alcoa derive from the special effort she puts into building strong relationships.

Teresa has attended my Leadership Academy seminar a record seven times in the last 31 years. Every time one of her client groups attends the program, she participates so she can better understand their strengths and weaknesses and so she can learn to fit in with the rest of her peers through the Team Building activities.

Teresa chose to tell me about her amazing boss Hanko Kiessner, CEO of Packsize International. As the story goes, Hanko came to the United States from Germany to study mechanical engineering. During his time in Utah, he fell in love with both the state and the woman who would later become his wife. Upon returning to Germany, he began to dream of a machine that could cut out the tremendous waste that occurs when companies ship things in standardized corrugated boxes.

After perfecting the design of such a machine that could make one-off customized-to-fit boxes, Hanko returned to the United States and set up shop in Utah. Of course, he wanted to make a little money, but his main goal was to contribute to his passion, the sustainability of the planet.

The founding concept of Packsize is "Building a healthy planet one box at a time." He has endeavored to build sustainability into every aspect of the company's operations. As part of this, he became one of the founding members of a Utah initiative, _For Clean Air_. The organization works on a pay-it-forward model where they will give any organization a free electric vehicle charging station if they promise to buy one for someone else. Packsize now has sixteen such charging stations on site to encourage his employees to switch to electric vehicles.

Hanko's compelling vision is "to not do business at the expense of others." You can imagine how powerful of a hook that is in recruiting talent to the organization. His personality is a second draw. Teresa describes Hanko as a leader that makes everyone he comes into contact with feel special. He coaches in a way that is uplifting rather than deflating. Teresa says that Hanko is the humblest and most self-aware leader she has ever met. He lights up a room with his smile and boundless energy. He places heavy emphasis on the hiring process refusing to settle for "B" players despite yearly growth approaching 40 percent, which of course requires them to hire more people.

When a vision that resonates with people is combined with an electric personality, it is no wonder that Packsize is quickly becoming a Utah legend.

CHAPTER 5

STRATEGY FOUR - USE TRUST AS THE GLUE THAT CEMENTS RELATIONSHIPS

"From an evolutionary perspective, it is critical to our
survival to know whether a person deserves our trust.
Competence is only valued after trust has been established."

Harvard Psychologist Amy Cuddy

WE SEE IT all the time: Wealthy, powerful, educated, or sophisticated people in leadership positions crashing and burning in spectacular fashion after years of success. Some are breathtaking in their stupidity, such as the overnight demise of CIA Director General David Petraeus, Congressman Jesse Jackson, Jr., or Speaker of the House Dennis Hastert due to betrayal of trust.

Volkswagen CEO Martin Winterkorn was forced to resign after acknowledging that 11 million VW-made cars had software designed to dupe official emission tests.[1] Dov Charney, CEO of American Apparel, was fired after allegations surfaced that he had misused corporate funds and sexually harassed employees.[2] In November 2016, Rio Tinto terminated two of its top executives for "failing to maintain the ethical standards expected of them."[3] Wal-Mart CEO Mike Duke was asked to resign amid bribery

DR. JOHN W. HANES

allegations.[4] Waste Management reported $1.7 billion in fake earnings and chose to pay $457 million to settle a class-action suit for fraud.[5] In the Veterans Administration hospital scandal of 2014, it was determined that a large number of employees falsified records to meet VA targets.[6] It was even worse at Wells Fargo, who fired 5,300 employees and was fined $185 million for creating tens of thousands of fake accounts to meet aggressive goals.[7]

The Wounded Warrior Project fired two of its most senior executives over lavish spending.[8] In the period from 2010 to 2016 alone, hundreds of elected officials at the state or local level were convicted of breach of trust crimes.[9] A 2015 study conducted by the US Army War College concluded, "The Army culture is rife with dishonesty and deception at all levels of the institution."[10]

In Major League Baseball, the Mitchell Report pointed the finger at eighty-nine players that were said to be illegally taking performance enhancing drugs. NASDAQ Chief Bernard Madoff plead guilty to bilking thousands of investors out of billions of dollars in one of the largest Ponzi schemes in history. Former ImClone CEO Sam Waksal served jail time for securities fraud. Religious leader Jim Bakker of the PTL ministry fleeced his own flock. The world is filled with people of questionable character who somehow ascend, at least for a time, to positions of power.

The blizzard of breach of trust scandals over the past few years has caused many people to simply *expect* their leaders to lie, cheat, steal, act immorally, or otherwise abuse the power of their positions. As a result, most people tend to place their trust in others more grudgingly than ever before. A Time Magazine/CNN poll found that 71 percent of people believe "the typical CEO is less honest and ethical than the average person."[11] A recent study conducted by Tolero Solutions found that 45 percent of the people surveyed say that lack of trust in their organization's leaders is the biggest issue impacting their work performance.[12]

Taking the time to establish a basis of trust with followers would seem to be common sense, but sadly it is not common practice. Some leaders are simply too busy. Others think that their associates will trust them because of their position or until they do something untrustworthy. A few come across as inauthentic, failing to realize how they are perceived. Yet, if a level of trust can be established, it can serve as currency that will allow the leader to pursue his agenda more aggressively and effectively.

Ten Habits of Trustworthy Leaders

Habit One – Act with Authenticity

All leaders have two selves – the inner self and the outer self. Authenticity can best be defined as consistency between the two selves. The notion of a person being "for real" means that phoniness is virtually eliminated.

Leaders often mistakenly believe that leadership is about playing out a scripted role, adopting a persona, or delivering well-written speeches. Many are tempted to think their power to move people in the desired direction derives from the size and location of their office, the impressive-sounding title they have been given, or the tricks they can learn about Machiavellian manipulation.

Aspiring leaders search for what they believe will be the holy grail of leadership, a checklist of traits they can develop and cross off the list on their way to the Ivory Tower. After a lifetime of studying, working with, consulting to, and coaching executives, I believe the strongest leaders are all about authenticity. It starts with knowing yourself and developing into the best self that your natural gifts and hard work will allow you to become. It is about character and lasting relationships.

Indispensable Tip

Former Medtronic CEO Bill George believes authentic leaders draw inspiration from their own lives to develop their own unique leadership style. He defines authentic leadership as understanding your purpose in life, practicing your values, leading with your heart, establishing connected relationships, and demonstrating self-discipline.[12]

Many leaders do know themselves but fail to appropriately disclose their shortcomings to others. Over the years, I have advised thousands of leaders at all levels to go public with the results of the 360-degree feedback they receive in my seminars. By my estimation, about one in five actually follow through and do this when they return to work. What makes this shocking is the leaders' direct reports are the ones who gave these people the insight about their weaknesses in the first place – they already know. All they are looking for is an admission from the leader.

Now, as you might expect, weaknesses are best disclosed after leaders have demonstrated their competence, skill, and developed something of a positive track record. This disclosure doesn't need to be a bare-your-soul issue of *"true confessions."* No one wants to work for a self-flagellating loser. And, it would be a huge mistake to dwell on one's weaknesses in the midst of a crisis.

Dave Schlotterbeck, then CEO of Alaris Medical Systems, went public with the results of his 360-degree evaluation in front of his top 130 managers at their annual Global Leadership Forum in Palm Springs. Up until then, Dave was generally regarded as a bottom line, take no prisoners executive. As he spoke, you could have heard a pin drop. The people in the room were both mesmerized and inspired. Then one by one, his direct reports, none of whom had planned to share their results with the group, stood and followed Dave's lead. It was a seminal event in the organization's history, creating a collective bond that remained for years. It led to the company adopting a core value of transparency and began Dave's emergence as a *leader*. Michael Dell did the same thing via a worldwide video conference to all Dell managers and received hundreds of e-mails praising his courage and honesty.

Many forgive General Petraeus's human weaknesses, President Donald Trump's sometimes brash and crass style, and Dallas Mavericks owner Mark Cuban's outlandish tirades because we sense they are genuine people, passionate about something they care deeply about.

There is something disarming about a leader who is not afraid to speak candidly. There is a magnetic attractiveness to someone who possesses conviction. Combine the two and a leader can light up a room despite underwhelming platform-speaking skills.

Far too few leaders are willing to take the risk of opening themselves up around their people. They have yet to learn the secret that making an emotional connection is often more important than their exact choice of words. They simply don't "get" the contagious nature of personal passion.

Habit Two – Be Visible and Available

It's unlikely that we will trust someone we do not know. It is difficult to know someone we seldom see. Plenty of executives give lip service to "leading by example" or the importance of being "visible," but most let more pressing events keep them from actually doing it. It has been my experience that associates at all organizational levels want to judge for themselves the capabilities and compassion of their leaders. They want to know that their leader can be trusted and that there is a firm hand guiding the enterprise. None of this can be accomplished if a leader hides behind closed-door meetings, a stack of reports, or a massive desk and manages remotely through e-mail, cell phones, and Twitter.

From the leader's side, not being on the scene often causes them to be cut off from critical insights and perspective, which can often only be gleaned from "being there." It has been documented many times that much of the failure of disgraced former Federal

Emergency Management Agency head Mike Brown during Hurricane Katrina was due to his being nowhere near the Gulf States during the crises, trying to manage remotely.

Where a leader spends his/her time sends an unmistakable signal that the activity is highly valued. When Bill Marriott Jr. visits more than 300 of his company's hotels a year, he is shouting out loud and clear that there is no substitute for being out in the field where the action is. When Oscar Munoz took over United Airlines in early 2016, it had the worst ratings of any legacy carrier in such things as on-time arrivals, baggage handling, and customer satisfaction. In less than a year, all these measures have improved dramatically. He did it largely by placing himself on the front lines. He had meals with the mechanics, ramp personnel, reservation agents, and flight attendants, which made up the bulk of his airline. He visited every major airport as often as he could and provided the example to his staff that it would be a good idea for them to do it too. He listened, he watched, he coached, and he inspired. He gave an important face internally to the enterprise. He also created trust with the unions by agreeing to a generous new contract that had been unsettled for years.

Disney Chief Bob Iger drops into the Imagineering Studio unannounced to sit with associates and discuss their challenges and ideas. He has said on numerous occasions that some of the best ideas he ever had percolated up from those impromptu get-togethers. He regularly walks the theme parks to get a sense of what is and isn't working. He minimizes sitting through the endless formal business presentations that came to define leadership at Disney before his arrival. Iger and Marriott are among the most trusted business leaders of their generation. And Munoz is off to a great start at reestablishing trust at United.

Leadership Tales from the Workplace

I was asked to conduct a strategic planning retreat with the top executives of one of the nation's largest and best-know theme parks. One by one, they presented volumes of studies and statistics on everything from the average wait time at each major attraction in the park to the sales-per-hour of every restaurant or hotdog cart on the property. Yet, when questioned, most of these executives seemed to have very limited depth of understanding of the fundamentals of their part of the operation. They knew *what* was going on, but they seemed to have no clue as to *why*. Worse, they had only vague ideas about what to do in the future to solve a problem or capitalize on an opportunity. They did, however, seem surprised when the results of the companywide employee opinion survey indicated that they scored low on trustworthiness. Finally, it dawned on me to ask them how much time they spent each day walking the park. To my astonishment, the largest amount of time *any* of these executives committed to this activity was ten minutes, and even he admitted that was only because that was the time it took him to walk to his office from the parking lot and back. How on earth can you successfully develop trust or run a business where virtually all of your associates touch the customer in some way and you never spend time with them?

At the minimum, a leader has a responsibility to be available to his/her followers. But so much can be gained from being out in the nooks and crannies of the operation and so much can be lost if one is not visible.

Tales from the Workplace

When my friend, Fred Howard was CEO of Metagenics, he would at least once a day walk around the facility to catch up with people, listen to their ideas, hear about obstacles they were facing, or just take the pulse of the place. He would deliberately walk the same route through the warehouse, customer care, sales, finance, etc., setting himself up to get "ambushed." His associates knew they had access to his ear if they had an issue. Fred made it clear to his direct reports that in no case would he use this information as a way to undermine the chain of command. This was an extremely important nuance to avoid creating undue anxiety among his staff. And, if he was out and about and happened to make a decision in one of his people's areas, he would immediately inform them of what he had done and why.

Interestingly, one day Fred overheard an associate talking about this practice and referred to it as a "Fred By." He thought to himself, "Oh no, that cannot be good." So for a period of a few weeks, he stopped walking around the facility. When one of his staff asked why he no longer visited each department, he replied, "I got a sense people were making fun of the practice, calling them Fred By's, so I stopped." His staffer shot back, "Are you kidding, everyone loves the opportunity to share ideas with you that have not been fully vetted or prepared properly. It electrifies them to know that you care about them and they think it is fantastic that you take the time to do it."[13]

A Tale of Two Leaders

Some years ago, a 2,500-person manufacturing company hired a new president from outside the industry to run the company. He had one of the most impressive resumes a 32-year-old fast-track superstar could have ever assembled. PhD in nuclear engineering from one of the finest universities in the country, White House Fellow in his mid-twenties, division vice president of a major company at 28, and a Mensa-level IQ of nearly 170 – the whole nine yards. This company had a strained relationship with its union for years, which did not get much better during his tenure.

During the next five years, he became seen as aloof, uncaring, and unapproachable. He seldom set foot in any of the numerous manufacturing cells in his company. In fact, most could recall only his initial orientation tour and a few times when he wanted to film a presentation with machinery running in the background as a backdrop. Grievances and turnover went up, and the number of employee suggestions went down.

After a few years of mostly large losses, he was replaced by a leader with a style 180 degrees different. The leader's IQ was probably significantly lower, and he possessed a bachelor's degree instead of a PhD, but within a matter of months he was able to generate incredible rapport with the rank and file of the union.

Each Monday morning, the new leader would begin his day by getting onto a flatbed electric cart that had a massive coffee urn on the back. He filled the remaining space on the cart with 10 dozen doughnuts that he would purchase on his way to work. For the next couple of hours, he would drive through the manufacturing facility, inviting the hourly associates to stop work for a few minutes and join him by the cart.

The first time this fellow would hit an area, he would require each person to shake his hand and tell his name before they could get the free coffee and doughnut. As you might imagine, given the previous president's style, they thought this was some sort of publicity stunt, and surely they would never see him again. To their amazement, he not only reappeared the next week, but also remembered most of their names. He then proceeded to ask them about their families, hobbies, and life outside of work. When he showed up the third straight week, he would ask how their daughters were doing in Little League or whether their sons had recovered from the flu.

After several weeks of generating comfort and building trust, the new leader began to probe into more substantive issues. He would get their thoughts on problems they were experiencing, quality or equipment issues, or simply any ideas they thought might be worth pursuing. In addition, it became known that he and his wife had a tailgate party in section J-5 of the stadium parking lot during the local NFL team's home games. *Anyone* from any part of the company was invited to stop by to share some refreshments.

Perhaps not coincidently, there were few labor issues, the contracts that came up for negotiation during his tenure were resolved amicably, and there were a record number of associate suggestions each year. A few years later, the new leader leapfrogged over the former to become CEO of their Fortune top 50 percent company, where he went on to lead them to record profitability. The sad part is that the former leader exhibits one of the highest levels of honesty and ethical conduct of any executive I have ever gotten to know. But because of his invisibility, few others ever got to see that side of him. Garnering trust, it seems, takes much more than simply being of high character.

Habit Three – Using E-mail Properly

Watching a typical manager work today, you would think you were looking at the control room operator of a nuclear power plant. Hours upon hours spent staring at a plasma screen display sending and responding to e-mails seems to be de rigueur for today's techno-savvy managerial class.

Management by e-mail is a fact of life, but it seems the pendulum has swung too far regarding its place in a manager's repertoire of tools. E-mail was designed to complement face-to-face interactions, not substitute for it. Today, it is not that unusual to see a manager holed up the entire day in his or her office pounding out an endless stream of e-mails. I once had a participant in my seminar that admitted to sending a record 500 e-mails in one day, and averaging a thousand a week. Not coincidentally, he received some of the lowest trust ratings I have seen on his 360-degree feedback survey.

E-mail is absolutely game-changing for sharing data between here and a location thousands of miles away. It is perfect for sending those odd-hour missives and directives when a visit or phone call would be out of the question. But I have to agree with Super Bowl-winning coach Mike Tomlin of the Pittsburgh Steelers, who said that inside an office, "Sending e-mails is the worst thing you can do. If you need something, walk down the hall and tell someone, so you are sure that what you want gets communicated fully and there is no misunderstanding. You cannot recover the wasted time that comes with someone later saying, 'Oh, that's what you wanted.'" U.S. Secretary of State John Kerry feels that despite all kinds of instant communication today, face-to-face contact is absolutely essential. It is a better way to deliver tough messages and allows you to take the measure of the other person.

Essential Knowledge

When you do choose to use e-mail, here are a few things to keep in mind:

1. People using e-mail tend to be less inhibited by social niceties and quicker to resort to extreme language and invective "flaming." It does not take many "shots" fired by e-mail to taint the whole relationship.

2. You lose the flexibility present in a face-to-face interaction. In a live encounter, the speaker can alter his communication in midstream if in reading the body language of the other person it becomes apparent that the message is off base. Face-to-face encounters allow for real-time interruption, feedback, education, and damage control. In essence, you can prevent possible mistrust from happening in real time when you are in front of another person. By the time you find out about the mistrust down the road through other e-mails, the damage has been done.

3. Associates who deal with each other primarily through electronic means find it harder to reach consensus and feel less empathy and compassion for one another. They simply don't have the same feelings of trust.

4. When you have a disagreement with one of your peers, resist the urge to copy your or their boss on the e-mail string. This is childish, guaranteed to incense your peer, and invites retaliation. It also burdens already higher-level executives with things they expect you to resolve at your level. This puts you in a bad light even if you turn out to be "right" in the battle.

5. Don't send e-mails to anyone while you are in a state of anger. Go ahead and write what you want to say but place it in the "send later" file. In a few hours, when you have calmed down, look at the e-mail again. Most often

you will be glad you didn't send it. Always remember that anything you write negatively in an e-mail can be forwarded to the universe and often is.

6. Avoid terse one- or two-word answers devoid of any tact. The ideal length of an e-mail is five sentences containing a single thought.

7. Answer *all* non-spam e-mails within 24 hours at the very least. Even if you just acknowledge receipt of the e-mail, you will be doing yourself a favor. It is absolutely unbelievable how many managers let hundreds of e-mails pile up in their system. It is the height of rudeness and incredibly arrogant to fail to respond to the legitimate requests of your colleagues and associates, not to mention the loss of productivity when people are waiting around for a response. If you really want to piss people off, don't respond at all. Unless you are Marcel Marceau, silence is not a good idea.

8. Don't send e-mail with a long distribution list if you are looking for a decision or response. The more people you send the e-mail to, the less likely any one person will respond or take action.

9. Remember that e-mails can be considered legally binding and used in suits and litigations. And as Hillary Clinton learned, don't use a private server for government business.

Habit Four – Accountability

Some leaders choose to moan about the lack of the organization's vision instead of creating one for their area.

Some leaders choose to compromise who they are by doing something they feel is unethical instead of taking a stand.

Some leaders choose to perpetuate a culture where people feel smothered instead of creating a model environment for others to emulate.

Some leaders choose to let poor performance slide instead of confronting it head on.

Some leaders choose to play the victim instead of making a difference in the things they can control.

Some leaders choose to expect their bosses to read their minds and know they don't have the understanding, data, tools, or materials they need to perform effectively.

The point is, in every case, *leaders* are accountable for the choices they make and the results they create.

It has been my experience that members of Generation X and Millennials in particular have developed something of an entitlement mentality. They seem to act as if the world exists to cater to their every need. As a society, we have made it too easy for people to duck personal responsibility. Lawyers can find loopholes in any contract. Bankruptcy laws almost beg people to file. People can annul a marriage years after the fact as though it never happened. It seems someone is always urging us to file a lawsuit when we feel aggrieved in even the slightest way. It is important that leaders stand up and be accountable for their actions. When they don't, they lose the trust and respect of their associates.

When Tom Peters coined the phrase, "It is often easier to seek forgiveness rather than permission," he was sounding a call for executives to step out and take charge of their areas of responsibility. I see reluctance to take action in the majority of managers who are sent to my seminars. Yet I seldom, if ever, hear the senior executives who sent these people say they wish their direct reports would take less initiative.

At Ritz Carlton Hotels, they have built accountability into their "Twenty Basics," which are down to earth guiding principles of associate behavior. For example, basic Number Ten states, "Each employee is empowered. When a guest has a problem or needs something special, you should break away from your regular duties and address and resolve the issue." Basic Number Sixteen says, "Escort guests rather than point out directions to another area of the hotel." They back these principles by giving every associate a large discretionary spending amount that can be used to solve guest problems on the spot. They encourage all associates to create as strong a positive relationship with customers as they can; even if it is as simple as asking if there is anything they can do to make their stay better.

This philosophy runs counter to what typical organizations do when they compensate only for individual performance, provide no discretionary spending authority, and write tight job descriptions that punish people for going outside their area of responsibility.

Job descriptions are necessary to create a set of hiring criteria. They also might work okay for low-level administrative or factory positions. But they create negative unintended consequences when used for knowledge workers. These jobs require a lot of judgment and the requirements for success change frequently. Skilled associates should be encouraged to roam and spend, within reason, to accomplish the task.

Accountability erodes when one or more of the following takes place on a regular basis:

"Head in the Sand," where leaders pretend there really is no problem or that it will simply solve itself.

"Scapegoating," where leaders try to shift blame away from themselves.

"Duck and Cover," where the norm is to document excuses.

Don't Forget This

The central premise of a culture of accountability is that it is a leader's job to eliminate things associates might use as excuses, reward accountable acts, and correct or eliminate members who behave in an irresponsible manner.

To create such accountability, there needs to be a shared purpose, trust, group recognition/rewards, and clear roles with both fixed and flexible boundaries.

Tales from the Workplace

When you think of skilled relationship builders, Ruby executives do not typically top the list. Then again, you probably have not met my long-standing client and friend, Karen Bomba, CEO of Morpho Detection. You would be hard pressed to find a leader anywhere who can match Karen's ability to win people over.

When Karen took the helm at Morpho Detection in the middle of 2013, the company was a bit of a mess. It was plagued by the trifecta of poor quality, late shipments, and lack of follow through in responding to and solving customer problems. One very large customer in particular became so exasperated with the company that they were on the brink of canceling their orders and taking their business elsewhere.

Karen's first move was to get in touch with the CEO and request a face-to-face meeting. Before getting on the plane for the visit, she did a little recon work to get insight into the person she would be meeting. To her relief, it was apparent the CEO was a Ruby just like her. Schmoozing would be out, sincere apology with a commitment to change and solid plan would be in.

Since Karen was new to the company and not the one responsible for the problems of the past, her strategy was future focused. She would listen intently to the litany of issues the CEO was likely to raise, apologize for the company's past transgressions, and lay out a plan of accountability with specific milestones for action.

The customer was so impressed with Karen's open, honest, and targeted approach that he decided to keep his business with Morpho Detection. Karen changed the culture, hired a program manager to take responsibility for the client, and scheduled monthly progress meetings to keep everyone concerned in the loop. Instead of waiting for the customer to give her feedback, Karen took it upon herself to create internal measures even stricter than those the customer was using. They then pre-empted the customer by sending _them_ the measurements against targets so the customer never had to worry about what was happening.

Over time, the relationship became so strong that the monthly meetings became quarterly and eventually the client said, "You know what, let's not schedule any more formal meetings. You have followed through on all your commitments and I trust you personally to such a degree that if either of us have problems, let's just pick up the phone and talk."

Final proof of the strength of the relationship came this past December. There was a complicated matter of product exchanges, refunds, new purchase orders, etc. that under normal circumstances would have taken months of legal and financial documentation to cement a deal. It was in both parties' interest that the deal close by the end of the year, which would have been impossible under normal circumstances. But based upon the trust built up over three and a half years, both CEOs agreed to a handshake deal followed by a single page document of clarification to finalize the matter by the appointed date, with the more formal legal documents to follow months down the road.

The story illustrates how Rubies typically approach relationships. It certainly includes face-to-face contact and open communication but ultimately is about trust earned through a coherent plan, regular measurement, and performance to goals that forge the bond.

Habit Five – Transparency in All Encounters

Dr. Michael Burns, President and COO of Ferndale Pharma Group, has one of the best relationships with his board and associates of anyone that I have ever met. He is so beloved that even after Mike left the company to become the CEO of ReproMedix, a decision Mike later deemed to have been a mistake, the board chose to re-hire him as president of Ferndale Pharma Group. The organization's associates applauded the decision.

Mike says, "I was totally open with everyone that my decision to leave was a mistake. I wasn't embarrassed that things didn't work out. And because of the loss of face I suffered, it made people think twice about the possibility that the grass may not be greener somewhere else."

Mike believes in the concept of transparency with people. He attempts to ensure that associates understand as much as possible about the business. He goes to great lengths to explain to them why things are important to the enterprise and to them personally. He not only shares the organization's goals and plans with everyone but frequently asks associates in small roundtable discussions if these things are appropriate and realistic. He has learned when the company's demands of people are impossible, that's when people cut ethical corners.

Mike's most fervent belief is that forcing people to do things is never as helpful as getting them to embrace whatever needs to be done. And the foundation of creating trust is candor. He goes to great lengths to declare his motives and clarify his intent when he makes decisions or requests something from his staff.[14]

Don't Forget This

It is unlikely that people will trust a leader if the leader's motives are not known, misunderstood, or misinterpreted.

Habit Six – Respect the Boss's Needs

Every year, a few otherwise successful CEOs lose their jobs in large part for ignoring the care and feeding of their bosses, the board of directors. Perhaps it is the hubris that accompanies success. Maybe it is the fierce independent streaks that high-control personalities exhibit. Sometimes it is over-reliance on a personal relationship. Or it might simply be the failure to place communication with the board as a high time management priority.

David Crane at NRG Energy, Ron Johnson at JC Penney, and Carly Fiorina at Hewlett Packard are examples of smart people making mistakes with their boards. In Fiorina's case, by her own admission in her memoir, *Tough Choices*, she had disdain for the operational capabilities of her board and was continually "surprised by the advice and requests from its members."[15]

David Crane apparently did not feel it was necessary to get agreement from the board before going all in on "green" energy.[16] Ron Johnson reportedly got rid of sales promotions, cut brands, created new brands, eliminated "fake prices," bought back "fake prices," and reinstated sales promotions and coupons without even bothering to inform the board.[17] No wonder the directors lost faith in these leaders.

In pre-Sarbanes-Oxley days, boards of directors were made up of cronies of the CEO and, honestly, were not expected to know much about the inner workings of the company. They were for the most part expected to be a rubber stamp for the decisions of the CEO. Many did not even attempt to know enough about the organization to be tempted to offer meaningful advice. Consequently, it was probably dangerous to act on whatever suggestions they did make.

My, how times have changed. Now that members of the board can be held personally liable for failing to exercise diligence and shareholder lawsuits have become common, both the composition of the board and how members view their responsibilities are dramatically different.

Tips for Transparency with the Board of Directors

Respond quickly and courteously to requests for information, even though it may not be your highest priority at the moment. The people who can terminate your employment should always be a high priority.

Get in the habit of regular communication via e-mail, phone calls, or personal visits at a frequency level to their liking.

Be truly open to advice from the board. Presumably board members have enjoyed some modicum of success in their lives and careers. Perhaps there are critical pieces of insight that they are offering, but you have to be receptive.

If members of the board begin to roam around the organization taking your staff's precious time or changing staff priorities, you have to step in. You must make it clear that you run the business and that their violating the chain of command cannot be tolerated. Do this politely, but firmly, and tell them that you will be happy to provide them with any information they seek. It is amazing how disruptive it is when board members wander the halls and drop by the offices of your staff. It puts your people in a real dilemma as to how to respond.

For the most part, your job is to present solutions to problems you are encountering when dealing with the board. In a meeting, it is not a good idea to just toss a problem out to the board to get their reaction. They will most likely get the impression they hired the wrong person if you do this too often. Don't lose control of the meeting.

Tell them what *you* need to be successful.

One of a leader's highest priorities should be to create an environment of openness and trust with the people who are in a position to terminate their employment.

Habit Seven – Promote Ownership

It is much easier for followers to place their trust in something if they have been involved early in the process and been kept informed all along the way. In developing plans, selecting priorities, making decisions, and seeing to it that tasks are properly executed, few things are as important as "buy-in." But trust is reciprocal and involvement alone will not ensure your people will fulfill their end of the trust bargain. There are several reasons why employees fail to take ownership of their part in the process.

A common explanation is that they simply disagree with a leader's course of action altogether. These people can create real trouble because their inclination is to openly resist anything related to the action expected of them. Worse, they may even go so far as to enlist others who share their views in their "resistance movement." People like this will look to bail out of the process at the earliest opportunity. The best approach to take with someone who disagrees with a decision is to first try and educate them on the merits of the decision or reasons behind the course of action. If, however, the person fails to "get it," then he must be moved into a position where he cannot block the actions of others.

A second cause of failure to take ownership is because associates see themselves as being overloaded by other tasks. People like this might even agree that the action required of them by the leader is a good thing; it's just that they feel "swamped." Periodically, taking things off people's plates will work best here. Failing that, it is imperative that the leader clarify to the employee and all others who may be affected that the work he is requesting is of the highest priority.

> ## Indispensable Tip
>
> Everyone is overloaded with work these days. So many things people are asked to do add very little value. At least once a quarter, every associate should be allowed to suggest items to be taken off their plates. You will get far more buy-in to the tasks that remain.

A third type of situation leaders encounter is where people put forth a token effort to comply with the tasks expected, either out of loyalty to the leader or a sense of professionalism. Attempting to win the "hearts and minds" of these people through inspiration is the key. Three of the best ways to accomplish this are showing associates that they play a key role, creating as much involvement for people as possible, and allowing some flexibility in terms of the latitude they are given to structure the tasks in ways they find desirable.

Tales from the Workplace

In *The Art of Possibility,* Benjamin Zander, conductor of the Boston Philharmonic, says that he came to a startling realization one day after he had been conducting for nearly twenty years. It dawned on him that while the conductor graces the cover of the orchestra's program, he does not personally produce a sound. His success derives solely from enabling the musicians to play each phrase as beautifully as possible.

Even though an orchestra is one of the last bastions of truly autocratic leadership, Zander thought it best to break tradition and give his players a voice. He initiated a ritual of placing a blank sheet of paper on each musician's stand before every rehearsal. They were invited to write down any observation that might allow them to play the piece more beautifully. When he would adopt a player's suggestion, he would make eye contact and nod at the proper moment to the musician responsible for the improvement, thus turning it into *their* moment.[18] Needless to say, both the performance and the buy-in were enhanced.

One of my favorite phrases is, "Change done to you is stressful and debilitating, while change you choose is liberating and growth producing." It is truly amazing how much pain people will tolerate if it is their choice and equally amazing how little pain they will tolerate if it is forced upon them. Too many managers make the mistake of planning everything for their people down to the smallest detail, thus disenfranchising them in the process.

A fourth reason people resist taking ownership is that they fear the consequences of failure more than they value the benefits of success. Dr. Denis Waitley tells the story of placing a two-foot-wide piece of wood on the ground and asking a person to walk across the beam. If they are successful, they get $20. Of course, no one balks at taking that challenge, as there is very little likelihood they will fall off the beam, and even if they do, the consequences are not very severe. However, when that same beam is placed on top of a multi-story building, very few people choose to walk across for the same payoff. They now are driven almost entirely by fear. For these types of situations, the leader either needs to greatly increase the reward for success or reduce the penalty of failure.

The final reason people passively or aggressively resist doing what is expected of them is that there is no real penalty for failing to comply. In an oft-told story about parachute packers, supposedly they felt great about achieving a quality level of 99.9 percent. Then again, they just packed the chutes, they did not have to jump themselves. Of course, one paratrooper out of a thousand didn't think that number was too impressive since if their chute failed to open it would result in death. So the commander changed the system. Once a week, the packers would make a jump with the parachute they wore picked at random from those packed the week before. The error rate promptly went to zero. This is what happens when "buy-in" is taken to heart instead of merely being a slogan.

What "buy-in" does is increase the overall *effectiveness* of decisions. The quality of a decision, multiplied by people's commitment to implementing it, determines the overall effectiveness of the decision. Suppose that you make a perfect ten decision on a ten-point quality scale, but the commitment of the people to implement it is a two. The result is a decision that scores twenty on the effectiveness scale. But, suppose the quality of the decision is an eight and people's commitment to implement it is also an eight. You get a score of sixty-four on the effectiveness scale or more than triple the effectiveness of the so-called perfect decision. The quickest way to up the commitment part of the equation is through involvement.[17] As they say in the military, "Soldiers who are active in planning the battle seldom battle the plan." In essence, we are more likely to trust something that we are involved in creating.

Habit Eight – Trust Others in Order to Become Trusted in Return

One executive I worked with years ago would stand at his office window each morning taking notes as to what time various people arrived. Yet he never bothered to see what these people were accomplishing. In his mind, if they weren't in the office at least an hour before the official starting time, they weren't dedicated.

There are so many occasions when salaried associates work late into the evening, travel for the organization on their own time, or work weekends that it is a frustrating waste just to put in face time. Essentially, we need to show our people that we trust their judgment as to how they allocate their time to accomplish their key tasks.

Cali Ressler, Jody Thompson, and Brad Anderson of Best Buy have gone one step further. In the book, *Why Work Sucks*, they describe the "results-only" work environment they created together at Best Buy.

A key premise of their system is that results against expectations should be the thing that counts most in the organization. They advocate a radical overhaul of the culture of enterprises as it relates to things like time spent on tasks and physical presence at work. Their approach goes well beyond alternative work arrangements like telecommunicating. It attempts to put to rest cherished but wrong-headed notions that organizations should reward effort or how many hours a person works. Amen! In a knowledge economy, it should be all about results against expectations.

In the "results-only" work environment, people are trusted to work from whatever location they want and put in the hours they desire, as long as they meet all their objectives. The culture does not ostracize people for coming in late or leaving early. There is no attempt to pile on more work if an associate finishes work early and wants to leave.[19] You can imagine the sense of being trusted that people working in such a system feel.

At Netflix they have gone even farther than Best Buy. They have an unlimited vacation policy where with a few exceptions, salaried workers can take off as often as they would like as long as their work gets done. They also have an expense reporting policy that consists of five words – Act in Netflix best interest.

The company view is that they hire exceptional people that are not only worthy of freedom, but thrive on it. Then they have a culture that rewards the high performances while weeding out chronically low performers. In the words of their CEO, "We don't want people inhibited by a myriad of rules. We allow them to be the best version of themselves."

Tales from the Workplace

John Rae, Vice President at Cleveland Golf/Srixon USA, shared a story with me as to how a change in perspective and the development of deep personal relationships served to overcome a massive trust barrier.

Several years ago, Cleveland Golf in Huntington Beach, CA, was acquired by Srixon Golf in Japan. In many mergers, the idea is to eliminate duplication of effort by combining functions such as research and development, marketing, human resources, and the like. Of course, leaders of the acquired company often worry about whether they will still have jobs, so on the Cleveland Golf side, there was palpable anxiety. On the Srixon side, they sensed this and quickly sought to alleviate the worry by announcing that each of the companies would continue to run their own functions, but there was a catch. Each function would have to coordinate its efforts with those of their counterparts in the other country.

Initially, both the American and Japanese executives leading the functions struggled with trust. Neither side really understood how business was done in the other country. For example, the Americans did not realize that in Japan, subordinates always defer to their superiors, that meetings are held merely to confirm decisions that had already been made, and that the Japanese needed to have a deep personal relationship established over time before they can fully trust.

The Japanese did not get that Americans see meetings as a forum to solve problems, make decisions quickly, and often can form surface relationships based upon the task at hand, not necessarily on a deep personal level.

A lot of communication was done via e-mail due to both the time difference and spoken language barriers. The American executives saw virtually every communication as an attack. The e-mails they received were brief, harsh, and seemed condescending. The feeling was that the Japanese were questioning their intellect, abilities, and even their motives. The American response was to do as little as possible with their Japanese counterparts and find ways to strike back when they could.

Sensing things were not going well, both sides took action to build trust, though in different ways. The Americans hired a consulting firm to do some training on cross-culture norms and communication. One particular tactic the consultants used really opened John's eyes. The consultant had everyone write out an innocuous statement. Then everyone had to re-write the sentence using totally different words that had the same meaning. Finally, they were asked to write the sentence a third time without using any of the words in their first two sentences but which meant the same thing. To everyone's amazement, the final sentence was short and seemed much more aggressive. The tone and feel of the e-mail were both lost. The "ah ha" moment had arrived. The Japanese executives did not have the advantage of a full English vocabulary to make their points come across softer.

For their part, the Japanese executives invited the Americans to come to Japan. A great deal of time was spent together outside the office eating meals together, drinking, karaoke, and of course golf. By getting to know each other socially, the Japanese came to appreciate the unique talents and basic good nature of the Americans.

What started as a huge disadvantage—two companies clashing, has turned into a major strategic advantage. The company sells golf clubs to the entire world. Preferences and needs are different in each country. In the past, things would be designed and built hoping that what worked in one country, would work in another. By using the unique perspectives that each company can bring to bear on products, marketing, and the like, they no longer have to guess or hope, they know what will work better.

Habit Nine – Deliver Consistent Performance

A leader's credibility derives in part from her ability to deliver consistently superior results – past and present. This regularity of performance is what gives followers the impetus to trust that the leader will produce similar results in the future. Most people have come to realize that the best predictor of future performance is past performance.

The ability of anyone to routinely perform at high levels is due in large part to possessing the *requisite capabilities*. These are the knowledge, skills, attitudes, and style to do the job at hand. The perception of a leader's capabilities will be enhanced if she also possesses the degrees, certifications, and other credentials that serve to give independent testimonial to the leader's presumed capability.

When it comes to trust, track records matter. Warren Buffet gets the benefit of the doubt in trust-related disagreements because he has demonstrated ethical performance over time. Super Bowl-winning Coach Bill Belichick's track record guarantees him the underlying credibility to establish a basis of trust with new players quickly.

Consistent performers live up to their commitments even when it hurts. In "Winners Never Cheat," John Huntsman, Chairman of Huntsman Chemical, tells of a handshake deal he made with Emerson Kampen to sell a stake in one of his divisions to Great Lakes Chemical. The agreed-upon price was $54 million. For whatever reason, Great Lakes Chemical took over half a year to get the formal paperwork in order. During that time, the value of the stake rose by almost $200 million. Right before the papers were to be signed, Kampen called Huntsman and offered to pay half of the increase or $100 million more than what was agreed upon. To his amazement, Huntsman said no; they had a handshake agreement at the $54-million price and that is the way the deal would stay.[20] Now that is living up to a commitment!

To build trust through performance, credible leaders keep at jobs until they are complete. There are a lot of "starters" in this world. But there are precious few "finishers." Credible leaders seldom make the same mistake twice, are able to ignore distractions that derail others, and they take charge of situations starting to go poorly, well before the eleventh hour. These types of leaders let their results be their calling card, not their words. They realize that their trustworthiness is diminished if they don't deliver the things they promised. So they are extremely careful in the promises they make. The "average wait time" signs you see at Universal Studios while you are in line for an attraction deliberately state a longer wait time than will actually occur. They want you to feel good that you had a shorter wait than expected.

Habit Ten – Exude Ethical Honesty

We live in a world where it is difficult to hide anything from anyone for long. The proliferation of data available on the Internet has rendered futile most attempts to protect all but the most sensitive organizational secrets. Thus, adherence to the notion that it is the best to tell the truth has probably never been more critical.

Tennis star Maria Sharapova came clean as soon as she was confronted with evidence that she had used a banned substance. In terms of any lasting damage, the whole affair is pretty much a non-issue.

By contrast, Olympian Marion Jones denied for years that she had used performance-enhancing drugs, evidently including at least once under oath. Her prison sentence was due to the cover-up, not the crime. She learned the hard way that you can't talk your way out of something you behaved your way into.[21]

Drastic times often tempt leaders to consider cutting ethical corners they would never have dreamed of cutting under more normal circumstances. A small business owner in my community was faced with the prospect of bankruptcy. Instead of engaging her associates to help her come up with innovative ways to save the enterprise, she chose to get illegally creative. She asked each associate to file for unemployment claiming they were laid off. In actuality, her proposition was to have them continue to work full time. She would pay them the difference between unemployment and their full pay, thus cutting the business's out of pocket expenses for the same work. This is different than California's "Work Share" program, where partial unemployment benefits may be paid to workers who have their hours significantly reduced. Even if the business did survive, how could associates trust her again? How could she look herself in the mirror each morning with any kind of respect? Just imagine the stress she would have each day wondering if she would get caught defrauding a governmental entity. And unethical leaders give associates an excuse to rationalize their own dishonest acts.

Somewhere along the way, many leaders seem to have lost their conscience, this moral compass that provides insight into what is right versus wrong. The penalty for straying from one's conscience is guilt. There are only two types of people who are free from guilt. The first are those that follow their moral compass. And the second are those devoid of moral grounding. Given the steady stream of stories detailing the ethical lapses of leaders in all walks of life, it appears that many leaders have no shame – no moral compass.

Tales from the Workplace

Chris Carroll, Senior Vice President Human Resources of Callaway Golf, tells the following story. During the dot com boom around the turn of the century, the CEO of a high-tech company was riding high. The stock price was $150 a share and accolades from the media were pouring in like a flood. The CEO had always been something of an egotist, which others on the executive team felt they had to tolerate. It was the continual breaches of trust that they all witnessed that they couldn't stomach. One by one, they wrote the CEO off as untrustworthy. Sensing there was a problem on the executive staff, Chris hired a consultant to conduct a team-building retreat. One of the planned activities was a "trust fall," where in turn, each member of the team stands with their back to a double line of the rest of their teammates and falls backward into the line, trusting they will be caught before hitting the ground. The night before that activity was to take place, the CEO announced to the facilitator that he would not be participating as he feared that no one on his team would catch him. The next morning upon learning the news, a couple of others on the executive staff became so disgusted that they stormed out, effectively ending the team-building session right then and there.

Soon thereafter, the bubble burst on the dot com boom party and the company's fortunes rapidly spiraled downward. The CEO gathered his staff together and said, "We can weather the storm but we need to stay together and promise that none of us will cash out our stock. It will look like we are on a sinking ship if we sell our stock as we have to disclose any sales in our financial statements. The other executives agreed but unbeknownst to them, the CEO had already cashed out his shares and by the time they found that he had, the stock had fallen to $1.79 per share.[22]

Unfortunately, there is no simple, universal formula that details what is ethical. A leader's ethical system is his personal set of *ground rules* for making what he considers to be the *right* decision. There are four separate and competing ethical frameworks:

1. Conscience-based ethics as described by Martin Buber;
2. Social contract ethics of Jean Jacques Rousseau;
3. Rule ethics as popularized by Immanuel Kant;
4. The end result ethics of John Stuart Mill.

In Buber's view, ethics is defined by one's conscience. In effect, we can sense when we do something that is wrong and we experience a surge of guilt. By contrast, Rousseau would say the rightness of an action is determined by the customs and norms of a particular community. For instance, if it is common practice in a country that bribes be paid to facilitate business, then it is acceptable to pay them. Kant believed the propriety of an action is determined by laws and standards. In Kant's view, if it is legal, then it is also ethical. Mill purported that the morality of an action is determined by considering its consequences.[23] Obviously, there are plenty of times when one or more of these sets of *ground rules* will be in conflict. In a simple example, while I began this discussion with the idea that it is best to tell the truth (a conscience-based ethical framework), this might fly in the face of a *consequences* ethical framework that says that we should not unnecessarily hurt people's feelings.

My point is that a person of integrity is defined as one who makes an effort to use all four ethical frameworks. In practice, it implies that an effective leader, when faced with a consequential decision, consider the expected consequences, rules and laws, customs and norms of the community, and one's personal convictions, with the whole process grounded in common sense.

Perhaps the simplest test of all would be for a leader to ask, "How would I feel if my parents, spouse, and children were to read a story in the newspaper about the decision I made or the behaviors I engaged in?"

In the Internet era, everything a leader says or does becomes more closely scrutinized. There is an entire industry devoted to catching leaders' missteps. In an instant, a person's reputation can be enhanced or tarnished.

Trust is not built in a day but is built daily. And one false move can destroy all the goodwill the leader has painstakingly worked to generate. But making these ten habits the foundation of your daily work life will greatly increase the odds of success in building trust with others you lead or encounter.

CHAPTER 6

STRATEGY FIVE – AVOID THE SEVEN DEADLY
RELATIONSHIP SINS

> "It is fine to celebrate success, but it is more
> important to heed the lessons of failure."
>
> *Bill Gates*

Sin Number One – Arrogance

One quality that seems almost universally present in failed executive careers is arrogance. It is a major cause of insensitivity ("I am better than you"), unwillingness to delegate ("I am smarter and more capable than you"), betrayal of trust ("I can get away with it"), blind ambition ("I deserve it"), inability to work for a boss with a different style ("Can you believe I have to work for this idiot"), poor staffing decisions ("It doesn't matter who I hire as long as I am around to direct them"), and downward-only communication ("If people at lower pay grades were better than me, they would have my job and I would have theirs"). It seems arrogant people always need other people to look down on.

Don't Forget This

Feelings of low self-esteem (disliking oneself and feeling unworthy of good things) are at the root of arrogance. The arrogant person is desperately trying to mask internal feelings of unworthiness by projecting false bravado.

It is difficult to stay grounded when everyone is falling all over themselves to tell you how great you are. But somehow effective leaders manage to keep their true priorities in life straight. Jim Collins in his research for the breakthrough work, *Good to Great*, found that level-five leaders (the type at the helm of every great company he studied) "channel their ego needs away from themselves and into the larger goal of building a great company.[1] They seem to embody the Biblical notion of humility by thinking, 'But for the grace of God go I.'"

Humility involves respect for others, but it should not be confused with weakness. *American Express* head man Ken Chenault, *Nike* CEO Mark Parker, and *Xerox* leader Ursula Burns, are CEOs who are as mentally tough as any you will find. Yet they conduct themselves in a respectful and quietly assured manner.

Humble leaders see no task as being "beneath them," avoid seeming like a "know it all," treat everyone they encounter with respect, readily admit mistakes, and use self-deprecating humor. They go out of their way to mention and thank the people who contributed to their success.

In comparison, uttering racial slurs, telling ethnic jokes, demeaning someone's physical disability, sexual innuendo, and using a condescending tone are but a few of the things insensitive leaders sometimes do that get them into hot water.

Insensitivity factored into the black eyes suffered by the likes of Bob Nardelli when he was let go by Home Depot for trying to run a customer service business as a military unit, BP's Tony Hayward due to poor handling of the *Deepwater Horizon* oil spill, and former

Turing Pharmaceuticals CEO, Martin Shkreli, who was dubbed by the media as "the most hated man in America" after raising drug prices *5,000* percent. As Dave Schlotterbeck, CEO of medical device company, CareFusion (now Becton Dickinson), said, "It took me far too many years to realize that I never have to be disrespectful to get my staff to know that I want something done."

Lessons from the Workplace

Early in his NBA career, superstar LeBron James was generally regarded as a selfish credit hog content with winning individual awards. You may remember what I consider to be the most arrogant act ever committed by a sports star – booking a 75-minute live TV show on ESPN called "The Decision" to announce that he was "taking his talents to South Beach and joining the Miami Heat." Mind you, his former team, the Cleveland Cavaliers, who had paid him handsomely for the first seven years of his career, were only informed of his decision minutes before the show aired. Critics labeled LeBron selfish, heartless, and callous.

Fast forward to both the 2015 and 2016 NBA finals. After each game, win or lose, James made a point in front of the cameras to praise another of his teammates, whose contribution he considered to be vital to the team. He was widely lauded for his growth as a true leader in sharing the credit, even though it was readily apparent to everyone who knows the game of basketball that the Cavaliers could not possibly have won without him.

The funny thing about credit is the more someone tries to take it, people often say, "You were not that important." But the more someone heaps praise on others, people usually say, "We couldn't have done it without you."

A Quick Guide to Becoming More Humble

- Many people equate humility with thinking very little of yourself. It is really about having a proper assessment of your strengths and weaknesses. Leaders who have a realistic sense of self know that in every skill, there will always be someone better than them in that area. And to be a truly successful leader, you should seek those people out and tap into and utilize their greatness to accelerate achieving your goals.

- Do not focus inward thinking only of yourself. Spend your energy outward being concerned for others and their wellbeing. According to the American Psychological Association, this will allow you a better chance at forming cooperative alliances.

- Become thankful for the opportunities and recognition you receive, but be quick to realize that no one achieves greatness alone. Be effusive in giving credit to those who helped make your success possible.

- Realize that few people want self-absorbed, narcissistic friends, and they certainly don't want one as a boss. We all know the chronic bore at parties who talks incessantly about himself and his exploits, and we seek to disengage from them as quickly as we can.

- Consciously or unconsciously, we make judgments about others all the time. Try to catch yourself in the act of judging others and truly access yourself instead. Consider how you can improve instead of how you think others should act.

- Fess up when you do not understand or know something.

- It is okay to be wrong once in a while, and when you are, admit it.

- Listen more than you speak.

- Don't boast about your achievements, let others recognize them instead.

- Accept praise with a simple "Thank you, I really appreciate your noticing."

- Recognize that in most subject areas, you know relatively little compared to people who have spent a lifetime developing expertise in their field. The more truly exceptional people you meet, the more you realize how little *you* really know.

Sin Number Two – Being a Hater

It is a sad testament to the human condition, but I have observed that most people seem to need someone to look down on. Acting resentful, uncaring, suspicious, distrusting, and holding grudges would certainly seem to be traits that the majority of people would see as distasteful, yet far too often leaders act this way. It appears as though many people in leadership positions get so carried away with the power of their position that they tend to look for the flaws in just about everything and go around relentlessly shooting down others' ideas and opposing their positions. Sarcasm, cynicism, and negativity might be fine for "shock TV" personalities like Bill Maher, Rachel Maddow, or Bill O'Reilly, but they can be killers for the average leader.

Criticizing others is often futile because it immediately puts the other person on the defensive. All it typically accomplishes is to make the other person dig in and strive to justify their position and usually condemning us in the process. Any idiot can criticize and most idiots do.

A Tale of Two Princes

Once upon a time there lived in New York a beautiful princess named Tinley. She had many men who attempted to capture her heart but two handsome men, Sven and Erik were far more persistent and determined than the rest.

Unable to decide between them, Tinley sought her best friend's advice. "Both are cultured" she said, "both extremely intelligent and well educated, and one as much of a hunk as the other. Both were raised in a loving home by hardworking parents who sought to meet their son's every need. Both sets of parents sacrificed to send their sons off to prep school where they could learn social graces. Upon leaving prep school both Sven and Erik went to fine universities and each pursued and obtained graduate degrees in their chosen fields. How shall I choose?" Her best friend said, "Let's take a closer look at what they have decided to do with the gifts that have been bestowed upon them."

In a remarkable coincidence, while they were away at grad school both of their families received a sizeable inheritance. Sven and Erik were each given enough money that neither would have to work a day in their lives if they so chose. "So money would not be the deciding factor," her best friend said. Let's look a little deeper into what kind of person each of these men has become.

Sven realized how fortunate he was and chose a life of helping others. He was kind to everyone he met regardless of their station in life. He was gregarious and loved to engage people in conversation. He seemed to enjoy hearing everyone's stories. Sven looked for the good in others and tried to understand those things about people that he thought were annoying when he first met them. When life's inevitable difficulties arose he rolled with the punches. He had begun his career working in a not-for-profit institution dedicated to educating under-privileged children in the world.

Erik made no use of his fine education. After all, why work, he thought. I have plenty of money and someday I will inherit even more. Erik was shy and not a great conversationalist. He seemed bored when talking with others and seldom had much interesting to say, perhaps because he had precious few hobbies and very narrow interests. Upon closer examination Erik was a "hater." He seemed to find fault with everyone, especially those closest to him. Despite all his advantages Erik became easily frustrated by the everyday vagaries and tribulations in life. He took for granted almost everything his family and friends did for him.

"Wow," said Tinley. "I never looked at the two of them that deeply. Thank you so much for helping me see what should have been obvious. I am forever in your debt my good friend."

A Quick Guide to Becoming Less Critical

- Explore the reasons why you are too often critical of others or their ideas. Perhaps you feel that to be successful, you have to be right all the time. In fact, you will be more influential if you are perceived by others as open minded, flexible, and cooperative. In addition, you will get more done more efficiently when people feel comfortable sharing their ideas and concerns with you. Problems will be identified and solved much quicker.
- Withhold the urge to reject an idea until you fully understand it. Ask lots of questions. Ask for and offer pros and cons for every idea, not just the cons. Focus on listening first, then adding your perspective after everyone has spoken.
- At least once a day, go out of your way to sincerely praise someone for something meaningful they have done.

Sin Number Three – Acting Political

In my opinion, one of the many reasons why Hillary Clinton was defeated twice in her quest to become President of the United States is that she was widely seen as being blatantly political. Leaders in business can suffer the same fate. Those leaders who are highly political, tend to place more importance on appearances than they do on results. They seem to have a preoccupation with how they are perceived by others. Most are overly concerned with being seen as popular. The typical political leader has difficulty with confrontation or conflict. They go to great lengths to cover their rear ends and avoid accountability when things go wrong. They say what others want to hear versus what they really believe. When a decision is called for, the highly political person will procrastinate and do as much as they can to avoid deciding. They are seen as wishy washy, lacking in conviction, and easily swayed by others, especially their boss. Does anything on this list seem like something we should aspire to be as a real leader?

A Quick Guide to Becoming Less Political

- Realize that being political results in a loss of respect. Others usually realize when mistakes are made who was really at fault. Stand up and take the hit if you were wrong.
- As part of your weekly planning process, jot down any confrontational situations you are avoiding and why. Think of the potential long-term consequences of continuing to avoid dealing with the issue. Brainstorm ways to deal with the problem that will result in the best outcome for all parties.
- Voice your honest opinions more in meetings focusing on those areas where your knowledge, experience, and skills are the strongest. You are in your job for a reason and you have a basic responsibility to participate in communication and the problem-solving process. Accept that it is a fact of life that not everyone will agree with you.
- Enlist a trusted person to give you feedback when they hear you say things that might come across as political, or when they notice body language that might be perceived as pandering or appearing insincere.
- Focus more on results and less on appearances. As was discussed earlier, image is important but the results you produce will eventually trump image.

Sin Number Four – Frustration

Psychologists define frustration as dissatisfaction arising from unresolved problems or unfulfilled needs. We may love our work but at times we all have to deal with co-workers who annoy us, bosses who expect too much, and clients that give us fits. Things seldom go exactly the way we expect them to in life or work. That is both the thrill and disappointment in life. And as author Wayne Dyer says, "Needing to have things perfect is the surest way to immobilize yourself with frustration."

The root cause of much frustration is when we perceive people or things as being out of our control and keeping us from fulfilling our needs. It can be triggered by something simple like a product we just bought not working or another person who seems to "push our buttons." We begin to feel frustrated with our efforts because nothing we do seems to work. Frustration that is not dealt with can eventually lead to depression. We can react by trying to solve the cause of our frustration or we can simply give up. The clear message we should get when we are frustrated is that we should try doing something else. Too often people choose to react negatively to the distress frustration caused by becoming bitter, resentful, angry, or just falling apart.

Tales from the Workplace

Peter B. Angood, MD is CEO of the American Association for Physician Leadership (AAPL), the world's premier organization for physician leadership, education, and certification. The Association's mission is to help doctors gain the skills to assume leadership and management positions within healthcare organizations.

Dr. Angood is the perfect leader for AAPL. He was a trauma surgeon for many years before deciding that he would like to try his hand in a leadership role. Peter thoroughly understands the world of medicine from a practitioner's standpoint. Obviously as a trauma surgeon, he has the demeanor to work under pressure, but he is also a kind, humble, and respectful leader.

Spending his life in the medical field, Peter came to the conclusion that physicians are uniquely qualified to lead healthcare organizations. They have the frontline experience that gives them credibility throughout their organization and especially with other physicians.

However, Peter is a realist. He has witnessed firsthand that many physicians have underdeveloped interpersonal skills and are not exactly known for their sympathetic bedside manner.

The typical doctor is often seen as narcissistic, strong willed, and controlling by nurses and patients alike. And why wouldn't they be? Physicians are extremely bright, highly educated, and they routinely save lives. But these same qualities that allow them to be successful as a practitioner, do not always translate well in leading and managing in today's modern organizations.

When Dr. Angood took over AAPL, the organization needed a turnaround of sorts. Among other things the mission and vision were not clearly articulated. Consequently, the staff's daily activities were not properly focused. To Peter, it was clear that the association should be casting a much wider net influence wise. A great way to accomplish this, in his mind, was to reach out to other medical related associations to work collaboratively to improve the quality of healthcare leadership.

Peter got a rude awakening when he was continually rebuffed by several other associations. He ran into a brick wall of parochialism, turf protection, and narcissism. He became frustrated at his inability to get others to see what was so clear to him; that through collaboration, the entire healthcare community could win.

Dr. Angood dealt with his frustration in a very productive manner. He looked inward at himself. "Are _my_ strong-minded traits holding _my_ organization back? Am I really the humble collaborative leader that I think I am? Do I truly listen to my people in an attempt to understand?"

Like the lyrics from the Michael Jackson song, Peter said, "I'm starting with the man in the mirror." What an effective way to deal with frustration.

A Quick Guide to Reducing Frustration

- Set reasonable goals. Our goals should stretch us for sure, but frustration sets in when we continually fail to achieve our objectives.

- Change your focus to what you can control. Say your goal is to double sales; you cannot control that. What you can do is focus on the steps necessary to get more sales, such as making appointments with prospects, sending out proposals, or meeting more people through networking events.
- Instead of being overwhelmed by feeling you need to make fifty appointments to get more sales, concentrate on the one most important person to contact and make the call, not the other forty-nine.
- Do a self-assessment. What are the sources of your frustrations? Do you exaggerate their severity? Are you at all responsible for causing some of the things that irritate you?
- Let go of small annoyances quickly. Visit a hospital with terminal cancer patients, amputees, or paraplegics. Suddenly the things that irritate you will not seem so important.
- Adopt the US Marine Corps attitude: I will adapt, drive through it, tunnel under it, jump over it, go around it, and do what is necessary, but I will not be deterred.
- Be careful not to overload your daily agenda. Most people suffer distress when they don't get everything done that they wanted to accomplish.
- Few people want to work for a leader who lets frustration cause them to lash out at others. Re-read the section in this book about Emotional Control. Do what star athletes do – they channel their frustration into intensified focus.
- Read inspirational stories or watch movies based upon real situations where people have had to overcome great obstacles to achieve success. Hopefully such stories will inspire you.

Sin Number Five – Evasiveness

Evasiveness occurs when a person is intentionally vague or ambiguous and tends to ignore problems or shift blame. The root cause of evasiveness is an extreme fear of failure. Leaders who are evasive really are not leading, they are abdicating. They are consumed by what they can't or shouldn't do versus what they can accomplish.

Evasive people feel guilty not only over real mistakes, but also ones they might make if they were to take action. In leadership positions, they fail to focus the efforts of their associates. It seems you always have to read between the lines to get the true meaning of what they are saying. Evasive people are prone to talking behind others' backs and seldom confront problems quickly or directly. Their mantra seems to be "avoid risk at all costs."

Evasive people often delude themselves into thinking that problems others see really do not exist. When there is a clear problem, their first response is usually to define their role in such a way as to claim it is not really their responsibility. When it is clear that the issue falls within their area of accountability, their predictable response is to point fingers and blame others. Most evasive people in leadership positions become skilled at covering their tail through extensive documentation of their excuses.

A Quick Guide to Overcoming Evasiveness

- Roger Connors and Tom Smith in their book *Journey to the Emerald City* prescribe a four-step approach – See it, Own it, Solve it, and Do it. Seeing it means that you must first acknowledge that a problem really does exist. To own it is to take ownership of the issue regardless whether it appears in your narrowly defined job description. Solving it requires persistent effort as you encounter the inevitable obstacles that will occur as you attempt to fix the problem. The final step is to do it, to take action.[3]
- Accomplish one small task every day – especially one you would normally avoid.
- Set a goal to address things that bug or concern you within two days (if it is appropriate for you to address). Reframe complaints into an objective question like "Why do our staff meetings consistently take longer than scheduled?"
- Learn how to evaluate the relative risks of making a decision. Often the risk of not deciding is higher than the risk of making a mistake.

- Never talk behind other people's backs. If you have a problem with someone, summon up the courage to discuss your concern with them directly.

Sin Number Six – Toxic Rebelliousness

As Henry David Thoreau once said, "If a man does not keep pace with others, perhaps it is because he hears a different drummer." To be toxically rebellious is to be insubordinate, often defying established authority and norms of conduct. In the business world, it manifests itself as having a tendency to ignore rules and policies, showing disdain for the boss or co-workers, and being closed minded. Rebels have difficulty with compromise and accommodation. They often act as a "sniper" in meetings taking verbal cheap shots at their peers. At their worst, they can be the "cancer" on the team that makes everyone around them less effective. They seem to love to "rock the boat" and "stir the pot" at every opportunity.

It is easy to confuse toxic rebelliousness with being a maverick. In the business world, the maverick is often adored, where the rebel is vilified. Folks who are frustrated with the status quo see the maverick as heroes. Fred Smith of FedEx, Steve Jobs at Apple, Elon Musk at Tesla, and Richard Branson at Virgin are prime examples. The distinction might seem subtle, but the maverick brings other worldly talent, vision, and ideas that far outweigh any negatives their unique personalities might foist upon an organization. Whereas the toxically rebellious person brings far more problems to the team than they do talent.

Tales from the Workplace

Chris Carroll, Senior Vice President, Human Resources at Callaway Golf, has seen more than his share of executives whose careers flamed out due to toxic relationships with their peers. In fact, during his over 30-year career spanning several prior employers, he has had to get involved in the termination of half his peer group at the executive level. Seldom did these firings occur because they lacked the technical skills to do the job; it mostly came down to bad behavior. Chris shared two examples from a large company where he was previously employed. Both are classic examples of failing to heed the common-sense advice of being kind to the people around you when things are going well, because you may need many of these same people when things are not so rosy.

Chris told of a situation where the president of a large division was a smart guy who had a several-year run of making his numbers. Yet he was abrasive, blunt, critical, and totally dismissive of his peers in corporate support groups like legal, finance, supply chain, and human resources. The founder of the company basically turned a blind eye to this man's degrading behavior because he was making money for the company. However, the seeds of this executive's demise had already been sown. One year, the string of the division making its numbers came to an end. Almost immediately, the executives who this A-hole had run roughshod over banded together like a pack of wolves and presented the founder with a strong case as to why this fellow should be fired. This time, the founder acquiesced to their wishes.[4] It seems that you are only as valuable as your last performance, and when you are nasty and the numbers head south, so does your career.

Chris shared a second story where another executive of a similar temperament had abused his peers but somehow was able to achieve exceptional bottom line results. The company did the math and for a few years felt the good this executive brought outweighed the bad. Then one year the numbers fell into the average range. His group's performance was not bad, but it was not up to the stellar results of the past. Suddenly, even though his <u>behavior</u> had not changed, the <u>equation</u> did. The bad outweighed the good and he was let go, to the delight of his peers.

The bottom line is, if you want to do things that rebels do, you had better be terrific in your line of work. Otherwise, you will probably wash out.

A Quick Guide to Becoming Less Toxically Rebellious

- Before you go off and do your own thing, try and look for the reason a policy or procedure might have originally been put in place. If you understand past context, you might find there was a good reason that may not be readily apparent.
- Figure out which policies and procedures will really hurt you if you were caught violating them. Learn to follow these at all times.
- Seek frequent feedback from your teammates as to how they really view you. Do they see you as toxically rebellious or a maverick? You may be surprised that your behavior is not being viewed very positively by the rest of the team. You may be coming across as a spoiled brat or prima donna instead of the swashbuckling hero you envision yourself to be. There is a time for every strong leader to become a team player. Those that can't or won't are at best relegated to a "turnaround" role. At worst, they suffer a continual stream of penalties and frequent terminations.
- Realize that a downside to being toxically rebellious is that leadership and your teammates often ask themselves if you can be counted upon to be the good soldier at crunch time when everyone has to pull together. It is hard to lead if people cannot trust that you will be there for them.

Tales from the Workplace

One of the roles I play with my clients in the world of sports is to help them evaluate players for their fit with organization culture and team chemistry. As you might imagine, I come across my share of toxically rebellious types (think NFL draft busts

Ryan Leaf or Johnny Manziel) and maverick types (think New York Giants star receiver Odell Beckham, Jr. and Dallas Cowboy star receiver Dez Bryant). Before conducting my assessment, I always ask the leadership that is hiring me, "Is the player <u>currently</u> performing in the top 10 percent at their given position?" (i.e., quarterback). If the answer is no, there really is no point in my conducting the assessment. My advice is to "pass" on this player, as the bad they bring will certainly overwhelm the good, crushing team chemistry. If the answer is yes, this is where the challenge begins. Let's take the case of Dennis Rodman, often held up as the poster child for bad behavior. Prior to becoming a free agent, Dennis Rodman had a reputation for skipping practice on occasion to fly to Las Vegas to gamble. He would sometimes let his emotions get out of control and elbow an opponent in the teeth, garnering technical fouls in the closing minutes of close games. His constantly changing hair color, dress, piercings, and tattoos created a media circus in the locker room. He would sometimes defy the coaches' desire for him to play his position a certain way. All toxically rebellious behaviors. But, he led the league in rebounding several times and averaged seventeen rebounds a game in his prime. Clearly a top 10 percent performer at his position.

Phil Jackson, then coach of the Chicago Bulls, was thinking that adding a talent like Rodman would make it far easier for his team to win a championship, but he was afraid of the negative consequences that might occur if he were to add Dennis into the mix. His genius was to seek out superstars Michael Jordan and Scottie Pippin. He shared his desire and concerns with them and asked if they would be comfortable if there were a separate set of rules for Dennis that did not apply to the rest of the team. Jackson knew if the stars were supportive, then the rest of the team would follow their lead and not let Dennis become a distraction. And if they said no, that a separate set of rules would not be fair to the rest of the team, then his decision would be easy: No contract for Rodman. So, even if the rebellious player is a top performer, if the key players on a team cannot support unequal treatment, it is my advice that it is best to move on and not invite that behavior into the organization. By now, you all know the end result. Rodman was acquired by the Bulls and several more NBA championships ensued.

Sin Number Seven – Micromanaging Stars

Micromanaging in and of itself is not necessarily a bad character-istic to possess. After all, if your people are not very skilled and/or lack motivation, micromanaging will probably yield terrific results. But what kind of operation are you running if you have surrounded yourself with associates lacking in talent and commitment? Micro-managing becomes a career killer when you do it with your star players.

The two main underlying causes of micromanaging are either an overly strong need for power, status, prestige, and control, or an excessive concern for avoiding mistakes. In the former case, micro-management consists of a tendency to dictate matters rather than guide, a belief that force and intimidation are necessary to get results and a view that empowering others is a threat to their very position as a leader. In the latter case, micromanagement is a preoc-cupation with a level of detail that distorts perspective and judg-ment. It is usually accompanied by over analysis, procrastination, excessive concern with avoiding mistakes, and nitpicking.

In my 41-year career, I have consistently noticed that the two most common reasons why star players leave organizations is they no longer feel mentally challenged or they are managed too tightly. To successfully lead star associates, it helps to know how they differ from the norm, and they *are* quite different.

First, your star associates are difficult and sometimes impossi-ble to replace. As such, they have tremendous leverage. They are usually needed far more by their organizations than what they can be given in return. Many come to expect and some demand spe-cial perks and treatment. In the case of sports stars or Hollywood celebrities, they often make more money from commercial endorsements than they do from their contracts to play or act.

Second, many stars have pretty healthy egos and don't see themselves as working *for* anyone. In business, they often identify more with their *profession* than their organization. Because of this, they become well known in their professional circle, are well connected, and have seemingly endless employment options. Thus, your formal position power means almost nothing to stars. They need to feel they are choosing to be led. Stars will not make such a choice unless they have reciprocal trust with the person attempting to lead them. And, since micromanagement is essentially a lack of trust on the part of the leader, this core need goes unfulfilled.

A Quick Guide to Empowering Stars

- Examine your need for control. Those who covet control are ironically the ones who usually lose control over their stars. It is a leader's job to make the most effective use of their people's talents. If stars have limited latitude on how they should do their jobs, you are squandering a valuable resource. Figure out who is supremely talented and highly committed. Then give maximum empowerment to those stars you have identified. But, you must realize that few if any people are talented and committed across the board. Basketball star Shaquille O'Neil was great at rebounding and dunking, but a terrible free throw shooter.
- Every work day, ask one of your stars for their thoughts and ideas on a business-related topic. Thank them for their input regardless of what you think about their ideas. Implement those suggestions that make sense and acknowledge to others that the idea came from them, not you. This will show your stars that you confer special status on them.
- Recognize that your desire to micromanage may stem from your perfectionist tendencies. Perfectionism might also get in the way of meeting deadlines as well as frustrating

your stars. There are always costs to over analyzing and nitpicking.

- Acknowledge that whether something is perfect or good enough is very subjective. You may have one idea of how things should be done, but, does this match your stars' vision? If you are relentless in asserting your opinions of how your top performers should do things, you will turn those people off and cause them to leave or rebel.

- Whenever possible, it is important to deal with stars in person versus over the phone, in writing, or by e-mail. The visit itself shows the person that you consider them to be important. With stars, it often comes down to being respected.

- Leaders of exceptionally talented people should create opportunities where their stars can share their background and interests with each other. This can solidify their connection to your organization and show them that you care about their personal growth. Great people like to associate with other talented individuals. In sports, this is one thing folks enjoy the most about being selected to play in an all-star game – the opportunity to rub shoulders with those as talented as they are.

- Ask your star performers about their ultimate career goals. Do they want to become a CEO? Teach at a university? Open their own consulting practice? Write a book? Then, do all you can to help them take the next step toward *their* career goals.

- Challenge your stars to take a leadership role with others on the team. They may be able to accomplish some things with their lower performing peers that you can't as the formal leader.

Tales from the Workplace

A US Navy Seal Team is comprised of a varying number of members, depending upon the mission. In each team will be a couple of world-class snipers, demolition experts, and highly skilled recon specialists. Of course, each team has a formally designated commanding officer. Interestingly though, in a wartime scenario, the formal leader seldom leads. If the mission is to take out an adversary with a sniper rifle, the snipers plan and execute the mission with the formal leader reserving veto power. If the objective is to destroy a building with C-4 explosives, the demolition experts plan and take operational control of the situation with the formal leaders once again, having veto power. This fluid command structure allows for the optimum use of talent while still retaining control.[5]

CHAPTER 7

STRATEGY SIX – ACT PROFESSIONALLY AT ALL TIMES

"Being a professional is doing the things that have to be done, on the days you don't feel like doing them."

Julius Irving

THE NOTION OF being perceived as professional can be a critical component of achieving success in the business world. As with customer service, the absence of professionalism is frequently more noticeable than its presence. There are many things that can be done to allow oneself to be seen as acting professionally, or at the very least, not appearing to be unprofessional.

Professionals Show Up on Time Without Excuses

Being fashionably late might not hurt you at a social event, but it can be a killer career wise. We live in a complex world where it is impossible to plan for everything that can go wrong, so on rare occasions it may be extremely difficult for us to get where we need to be at the appointed time. Far too frequently, however, many leaders are chronically late for meetings or fail to show up altogether. Being such a leader with little regard for their own or others' time signals disorganization at the least and at worst a selfish, cavalier attitude toward work.

Over the years, I have seen many promotions to higher levels lost and on occasion witnessed leaders being fired for chronic tardiness. Time should be considered one of our most precious resources as it cannot be stored and it is impossible to buy more than the 168 hours per week that each of us is allotted.

Professionals Don't Panic Under Pressure – This is Often Determined by Self-Esteem

What causes pressure? Generally speaking, most pressure is self-induced, caused by how we think about ourselves, events, or impending challenges. The other major reason why people feel distress is situational in nature, such as how we interact with our environment. Common pressures include:

- "Do or die" games in sports
- Performing in front of large numbers of people (or a small number of very significant folks)
- Matrix management and its often-conflicting demands
- Unclear goals or lines of responsibility
- Conflicts with the boss, teammates, or family
- Overwhelming or impossible job demands
- Limited latitude or flexibility on how to handle problems
- Little or no recognition
- Geographic relocation
- Fear of failure
- Impatience
- Death of a loved one
- Divorce
- Upcoming vacations or the holiday season
- Major illness

The effects of these stressful situations can be magnified if we lack the proper support from our employer, boss, teammates, friends, or family.

How we handle pressure is closely tied to our level of self-esteem. Our self-image is the way we feel about ourselves. Self-esteem can cause us to feel more or less stress because it affects the way we perceive events. One's self image is largely determined by the impact our past experiences in life or business have on us today. A positive feeling of self-worth will allow us to make maximum use of our talents while poor self-esteem tends to set a low upper limit to what we feel we can achieve.

A negative self-image often results from internalizing negative things others have said about us or when people who are significant in our lives are overly critical. We develop a more positive self-image when people or events have caused us to feel important, valued, capable, smart, talented, and trusted.

People with high self-esteem have a sense of excitement about themselves and their future. They feel equipped to handle life's challenges. They accept what they cannot control and spend their energy on what they can influence.

Improving one's self-esteem begins by convincing ourselves that while we cannot change the events that shaped us in the past, we can change the way we view life going forward. If we continue to find fault with our skills, intelligence, or physical appearance, we will see everything in terms of our limitations of what we are capable of achieving. This negative view causes pressure.

Changing self-esteem is only possible when we begin to alter the way we think. For instance, if we grew up hearing people continually blame others, it is likely that we internalized a certain amount of this attitude ourselves. If our parents made all our decisions for us and attempted to solve all our problems as a child, we were probably not able to become fully self-sufficient. We most likely now find it difficult to make decisions later in life.

When a challenge in life occurs, instead of associating it with something in our past, we have to reframe the event to a "now" perspective. In a sense, we must say to ourselves, "What can I do based upon where I am today?" Psychologists refer to this as "locus of control." If we believe that chance or other people's actions determine our destiny, we have an "external" locus of control. People with an external locus relinquish their ability to influence outcomes. If we are convinced that it is what we do and not outside forces that determine our fate, we have an "internal" locus of control. Believing that what happens is caused by external forces puts the blame on others and causes us to feel pressure because we cannot control to any great extent what other people do. With an internal locus, we assume responsibility for how we act or the way we respond to the challenges we encounter.

Our level of self-worth is also a product of our need to have others accept us. People with a high need for the approval of others tend to sacrifice who they really are or want to be so as to put up the appearance of "fitting in" with whatever group they seek to be a part of.

The causes of a high need for acceptance are usually associated with an absence of feeling loved as a child. To try and capture love, many children focused too heavily upon whatever seemed to win the approval of anyone of significance – parents, teachers, or friends. For many, this hardened into a lifelong pursuit of the love of others. Once again, since we cannot control how others feel about us, we feel pressure.

To become more self-sufficient and less approval seeking, we must learn to love ourselves. This does not mean that we become satisfied with who we are, as we should always be striving to grow. But it does mean that we should not beat ourselves up over what we are not.

Don't Forget This

The famed psychologist Albert Bandura found that the more you repeat a destructive thought or action, the deeper and more automatic it becomes."

Once we become more self-reliant, we begin to see the difference between what we can and cannot control. We feel less pressure in crisis situations because we will focus on what we can versus what we cannot do. We will develop more effective coping mechanisms for those things truly out of our control. When we learn that it is not only okay, but also more important to please ourselves than it is to curry the favor of others, we will feel no pressure to try and always fit in. Or self-confidence will skyrocket and we will be relatively free from worry. The irony is that the more self-confident we become, the less we will care about what others think of us, yet we will gain more acceptance because self-assurance in a person is very attractive.[1]

Tales from the Workplace

A good friend of mine, the agent for one of the best-known actresses in Hollywood, asked me to do one-on-one life coaching of her as he explained to me that her career was in a death spiral. For years, this actress had been included in *People* magazine's "most beautiful" edition. Despite this yearly recognition, she had a hard time seeing her own exceptional good looks as she had internalized a very unattractive image of herself. While millions of people saw incredible beauty, what she saw in the mirror was a blemished face, gangly legs, a big nose, feet that were too large, and a weight problem. Movie critics added to her esteem issues when they wrote and she read that she had no acting talent and was only getting parts in films due to her sexy appearance.

As she grew older and some of her outward beauty started to fade, movie offers began to dry up. This created a crisis in her mind, and she began to have even greater doubts about her talents. When she *was* chosen to play a role, she would take quadruple the allotted time budgeted for her makeup. Camera crews sat idly by waiting for "the diva" to appear. Directors steamed, and it was not long before she developed a reputation as being difficult to work with.

The actress began to stay home, out of the limelight more often. Food was delivered to the house. On the rare occasion she did venture out, she went incognito, wearing a trench coat, large dark sunglasses, and a wig to throw off any paparazzi who might be lurking around. Eventually she became a recluse. And in Hollywood, out of sight is out of mind.

We began to work on changing the prism through which she viewed herself. We examined the thoughts that triggered good and bad images of herself. When it was good, we sought to reinforce it and when it was bad, we got rid of it or restructured it until it reflected something positive. We paid attention to how she dressed and made some changes to reflect her age. She practiced looking people in the eyes, voice projection, and got rid of the wigs, sunglasses, and oversized coats. She learned to see the paparazzi in a different light. They were just a few people with opinions trying to make a living and not worth paying much attention to. We enrolled her in some additional acting lessons, then set a goal for her to earn a part in a movie playing a dramatic role instead of sex symbol parts that had defined her career up to that point. Two years later, she played what turned out to be the role of her life and ended up *winning an Academy Award!*

A Quick Guide to Performing More Effectively Under Pressure

- Do whatever you can to put yourself in positions where you have the adequate support from others that will allow you better odds of success. Extricate yourself from people or organizations that saddle you with demands that are impossible to meet.
- Surround yourself with people who allow you to feel capable, talented, and valuable. Avoid those who continually demean you or your capabilities.

- Realize that while you cannot change the events of your past, you can move beyond them by looking to what opportunities your current situation presents. As someone once said to me, "You cannot get on with the next chapter of your life if you keep re-reading the last chapter."
- Develop an "internal locus of control" by accepting responsibility for how you respond to situations. It is usually not luck that causes our success; it is steady, careful preparation, attention to detail, and a relentless focus on execution, all of which are under our direct control.
- Use meditation or simply find some quiet time each day to calm yourself down.
- Do not add to the stress by ingesting substances that elevate your blood pressure like sugar, caffeine, nicotine, or narcotic stimulants. Reduce tension through exercise and isometrics.
- When you know ahead of time that you will be asked to perform in a high-stakes event, try and mentally walk through every aspect of the situation in advance. By rehearsing, once you get to the actual event it will seem routine.
- Examine your "self-talk." Are you losing sleep over how you might screw up? Focus instead on the great things that will happen when you succeed. Remember, winners want the ball!

Professionals Don't Air Their Dirty Laundry at the Office

Whether you praise or condemn San Francisco 49er Quarterback Colin Kaepernick for taking a stand against what he perceives as the oppression of African Americans in the United States, it is the general consensus that he chose to do so at the wrong place (his office, so to speak, in NFL stadiums) at the wrong time (during the singing of the National Anthem taking a knee). Indeed, voicing whatever grievances you may have against your family, your boss, your organization, your co-workers, or the world at large in your place of employment is not only unprofessional, it will usually garner you a fair share of detractors.

Former NBA Coach George Karl could have chosen to end his 38-year career on a high note and sailed off into the retirement sunset in grand style. If he felt he had to write a book, he could have spun tales of the greatness and other-worldly talents of the many gifted athletes he was privileged to work with. Instead, he chose the low road in writing *Furious George*, a tell-all tome trashing several NBA legends. The backlash was fast and filled with condemnation. If his aim was to sell more books, he may have succeeded, but at what price to his reputation?

If you have a grievance with someone or something, address it privately to whomever may be able to do something about it. Never gossip to others in the office. If you are the type of person who just can't keep things to yourself, choose a friend not connected to your work to dump on. Passing judgment on people you work with about these same people they work with is never advised. Your co-workers are smart enough to know that if you are talking badly about people in the office to them, that you are most likely trashing them to others.

Professionals Avoid the Appearance of Improper Relationships

Office affairs date back to Biblical times and continue to be an inevitable part of life in modern organizations. Mix attractive, powerful executives working extended hours in close quarters doing exciting work and this creates a potent cocktail indeed. Few things can kill morale and team spirit quicker than an improper sexual relationship. An example of the devastating effect this can have on a company occurred with one of my largest clients. The male CEO, who was married, was thought by his staff to be having an ongoing affair with the company's recently divorced female Chief Legal Counsel, who also happened to be in charge of Human Resources. The entire management team suspected the affair and talked about it regularly among themselves. Individually, each member of the executive team sought me out to explain what they perceived to be a major issue – none felt comfortable in working with the woman or even her two critically important departments because they feared everything they said would go right to the CEO. In addition, they all knew the CEO's wife and felt it to be terribly unfair to her as she had no idea something might be going on. When executives are disgusted with the suspected bad behavior of their CEO and feel they cannot trust their legal or HR functions, you can imagine the team dysfunction that ensued. Since I was an outsider and my work with the company was nearing an end, the executive team implored me to step in and do something. I confronted the CEO with the allegations (which he neither admitted to nor denied) and told him that either way, true or not, the perception of impropriety was keeping the organization from maximizing its potential. And if the board of directors were to find out about it, he may well end up losing his job and his marriage. And what if there was a relationship and it ended poorly, would the Chief Legal Counsel sue for sexual harassment?

When there is a perception of an improper relationship at work, the best you can hope for is to contain the damaging effects on the organization. Here is how it is done:

1. You cannot stick your head in the sand and pretend there won't be attractions. While you cannot legislate morality, it is the leader's job to make sure the relationship is mutual. When there is not mutual consent and you do nothing, you set the stage for lawsuits.
2. If affairs, married or otherwise, do occur within a department, immediately transfer the higher-ranking executive to another part of the organization. If that is not possible (which of course it wouldn't be in the case of the CEO), counsel the more senior executive to resign.
3. To reduce the appearance of improper behavior, a boss should never ask a subordinate of the opposite sex (or in the case of openly gay executives, the same sex) to dinner alone. If it is mission critical that such a meeting is necessary and

the subordinate is married, the executive should personally call the person's spouse and explain the situation. Perhaps if it is feasible, the spouse should also be invited. And it is not a good idea to invite a subordinate to the boss's home alone.

4. Bosses often have to conduct business lunches with members of their staff. When possible, a third person should be invited. The boss should be careful not to schedule such lunches too often with the same person.

5. Personal gifts from a boss to a subordinate should be discouraged unless all subordinates receive gifts of about the same value and with similar frequency. And make sure any such gifts are unlikely to be construed as having a sexual connotation.

6. If an executive is found to be using company funds to try to initiate or carry on an affair, the executive must be terminated immediately for cause. This would include the improper use of expense accounts, travel funds, unusual bonuses, merit increases, or promotions.

In the case of the CEO cited above, he in the eyes of his staff violated points 3, 4 and 5, causing a significant drop in morale and trust in both the CEO and Corporate Counsel. And because the woman also headed HR, there was no place these executives could turn to stop the problem short of throwing the CEO under the bus to the board of directors.

Professionals Produce Results Independent of Close Supervision

In any leadership position, taking initiative is a fundamental responsibility. Don't get me wrong; I am not saying that you should do anything illegal, unethical, immoral, unsafe, or insubordinate. But, someone has chosen you to lead, so run the show – don't feel you need to check everything with the boss. Too many leaders are so afraid of making mistakes or getting fired that they hesitate when key decisions need to be made or they overanalyze to the point of paralysis.

Instead of asking your boss to define your goals and priorities, set these yourself and review them with him or her to ensure they are consistent with his or her expectations. Create what you believe are the critical elements of the job that should be measured, being sure to define what you think exceed, meet, and failing to meet would look like for each measure. Share these with your boss to get concurrence. Then tell the boss what you think your current level of performance is for each key accountability to make certain that you are both on the same page. Finally, be sure to clarify the items the boss absolutely would like to be consulted on before you are authorized to take action. For everything else – run the show!

Tales from the Workplace

Mary Barra, CEO of General Motors, was chosen by *Fortune* magazine as the most powerful woman in business in 2016. Most thought she would never even be given a shot at the CEO's job because she was assigned to lead the Human Resources function. No CEO of GM had ever ascended to the top spot having served as head of HR. And frankly, the HR function at GM was a bureaucratic nightmare when she took over. Believe it or not, they had a ten-page policy of how to dress at work. Instead of accepting the status quo of inefficiency, she took the first of many steps to carve out what would be her defining legacy, tackling unnecessary waste and red tape. She took the ten pages out of the employee handbook, had her secretary build a small bonfire in the parking lot, and invited her peers to join her as she tossed the pages into the fire. The new GM dress code consists of two words – dress appropriately. For crying out loud, she said, "Do we really need ten pages to tell people how to dress?" Her entire time in HR was spent making similar decisions, seldom asking the CEO for permission.

Professionals Make Their Bosses Look Good – Not Bad

Regardless of whether you work for a supremely talented boss or one who leaves much to be desired, those who attain high levels of authority in life want to feel secure in their positions.

Endeavor to build a strong connection with the boss, but don't make the mistake of taking the relationship for granted. Just because you may be a favorite today should not make you feel that you can do whatever you want. I could write volumes about leaders who fell out of favor because they felt their relationship with the boss made them untouchable.

Tales from the Workplace

A few months ago, a billion-dollar client company asked me to conduct an audit of their finance and accounting functions. The CEO had become concerned that the Chief Financial Officer (CFO) was not up to the job.

The organization's corporate controller, a 20-year company veteran, had spent years cultivating relationships with the CEO and the rest of the executive staff. He became a master at the art of manipulation. The controller took every opportunity to flatter the staff, puff up their egos, and made them feel important by going over his boss's head and seeking out their advice and expertise in areas where he clearly knew what needed to be done. Over time, he began to slip little digs about the CFO into casual conversation, demeaning the CFO's intelligence, style, and capabilities. The executive staff became alarmed that maybe they had the wrong guy in the CFO slot, so they asked me to delve into the matter and make recommendations.

One by one as I met with the managers in the various functions, it became apparent that the problem was not the CFO, it was the controller. Granted the CFO was not all that skilled in emotional intelligence, but he was universally seen as brilliant, dedicated, ethical, well-schooled in every area of finance and accounting, and very willing to help his staff when needed.

The controller, while bright and not without some talent, had become egotistical, lazy, and selfish, openly mocked the CFO to anyone who would listen, and at times was insubordinate. A real cancer on the team. What had started as an investigation into the leadership of the CFO quickly turned into an indictment of the controller.

Tips for Working Professionally with your Boss

1. Get to know your boss's personality style. Is the boss a Ruby, Emerald, Sapphire, or blend? Understand their strengths, weaknesses, fears, and aspirations. Don't try to change your boss, learn to adapt.
2. Always communicate major ideas and plans before taking action. Most bosses hate surprises. Get in the habit of regular communication via e-mail, phone calls, or personal visits at a frequency to their liking.
3. Respond quickly and courteously to requests for information even though it may not be your highest priority at the moment.
4. When you disagree with a recommendation, suggestion, or directive from your boss, don't ever ignore it. Make a strong case as to why you disagree. Make sure that you both end in agreement as to what actions will or will not be taken. When possible, follow-up via e-mail or in writing to confirm your agreement.

   Despite the merits of your arguments or your perceived stupidity of theirs, avoid getting so angry that you publicly criticize the boss. You may burn a bridge that you will need later. And know when to stop fighting – beyond a certain point you impugn the intelligence of your boss.
5. Realize that some bosses are more insecure than others. If you are extremely intelligent, witty, charming, or more skilled than your boss, you may inadvertently outshine her/him simply by being yourself. If your ideas or solutions are

more creative or effective than your bosses, credit them to her/him in as public a manner as possible. Let others know that your advice is really their advice. If you are more socially adept than your boss, be careful not to make her/him seem cold and uncaring by comparison. If you are more intelligent than your boss, ask questions and find ways to get her/him to see the problem and possible solutions from your vantage point. Lead them to the answer in such a way as to allow them to feel they knew it all along. In each of these instances, letting the boss outshine you will keep you from being a victim of her/his insecurity.

Tales from the Workplace

In another large company, the current CEO was nearing retirement and two members of his staff, Kate and Sara, were each in line to be his successor. Kate was the older and more technically proficient of the two. Yet she was sorely lacking in emotional intelligence. Kate constantly belittled Sara to the CEO, undermined her authority wherever she could, and distanced herself from any collaboration with Sara.

Sara is a more emotionally intelligent leader and she chose to focus on doing the best job possible in leading her function. It was a close race as each of the two had the technical prowess to lead the company. Because of the age and experience difference, the CEO recommended to the board that Kate be chosen as the next CEO.

Instead of being magnanimous in her victory and realizing Sara was an incredible talent that could continue to enhance the fortunes of the company and by extension her own, Kate went a different direction. She further diminished Sara by reducing her role and continued to disparage her as a person. Sara seriously considered leaving the company, but she knew that if she just hung in there long enough that Kate's poor social sensitivity would lead to her imploding.

Almost immediately, the former CEO (by then chairman of the board) realized he had made a mistake in his choice. After just a few months, the CEO took the hit for his poor decision and convinced the board to demote Kate back to her old role rather than firing her. For the next several months, the chairman stepped back into the CEO role and Kate continued her antics. This time, the CEO recommended that the board choose Sara to lead the company, and they acquiesced to his wishes.

At this juncture, the board asked for my recommendation as to what should be done with Kate. After consultation with Sara and the other members of the executive team, it became clear that continuing to employ someone as duplicitous as Kate would get in the way of giving Sara the best chance of success as CEO. The board accepted my recommendation to give Kate a nice severance package as appreciation for her many years of dedicated service.

Professionals Avoid Falling into the Traps that Trip Up Amateurs

Amateurs Rely Upon the Gratitude or Pity of Others

When help is needed, amateurs too often hope that people will feel sorry for them and come rushing to the rescue, or because they have been helpful to these people in the past that the favor will be returned. Sapphires usually have a selflessness that will cause them to help, but most others will find reasons to ignore the request.

Professionals realize that pragmatism is a better approach. Most people do what they feel is in their self-interest to do. While this may come across as a cynical view, it is nonetheless how I have found the world to work. The pro attempts to get help by offering something valuable in return such as money, ego gratification, power, knowledge, connections, happiness, or even improved physical health.

Amateurs Believe that Whomever has the Strongest Argument Always Wins

Amateurs seldom appreciate that even when they have presented the better case and appear to have won the argument, they can never be certain how the other person really feels. Perhaps they will resent you and not take action. Maybe you have made them feel insecure. In the heat of the battle, you may have said or done something that has offended the other party and polluted the relationship going forward. As song artist Cher so brilliantly said, "Words are like weapons, they wound sometimes." Professionals realize that many arguments are fruitless pursuits. Instead, they create a demonstration that their idea will work. It is hard to argue against proof and there is no possibility of offensive words.

A renowned expert in the study of power, Robert Greene shares the following story from his excellent book, *The 48 Laws of Power* [2]:

A heckler once interrupted Soviet Prime Minister Nikita Khrushchev in the middle of a speech in which he was denouncing the crimes of Joseph Stalin. "You were a colleague of Stalin's," the heckler yelled, "Why didn't you stop him then?" Khrushchev apparently could not see the heckler and loudly barked out, "Who said that?" No hands went up. No one moved a muscle. After a few seconds of tense silence, Khrushchev finally said in a quiet voice, "Now you know why I did not stop him." Instead of arguing that anyone facing Stalin was afraid and that any challenge would mean certain death, he made the heckler *feel* what it was like to face fear and terror. The demonstration was so visceral that no further argument was necessary.

Amateurs Oversell

Amateurs think that if they just keep talking long enough and throw in every possible justification for their position, that they will eventually wear the other person down. They believe that a business presentation should contain virtually anything that might generate interest from each of the major personality types and should contain quite a few options to choose from. Professionals know better. Psychologist Barry Schwartz in his research for the *Paradox of Choice* found two unexpected things. Human beings get paralyzed by having too many options and the lower value words or items in a presentation drag down people's value of the good stuff. Professionals know that sometimes less is more, that listening is often better than speaking, and that occasional periods of silence where others can process what is going on will lead to better results.[3]

Amateurs are Afraid to be Bold

Being bold is not an always or never proposition. Being audacious all the time is exhausting and often offensive. But amateurs tend to accommodate others or seek halfhearted compromise solutions too frequently. They fear the consequences of bold actions that might fail without realizing the results of timidity can be much worse. They would rather be liked than respected.

Professionals have bought into the concept that fortune favors the brave. Interestingly, we often see bold moves in war where the consequences can be the highest. General Eisenhower's D-Day amphibious landing in World War II when others preferred a safer route or a postponement for better weather; General MacArthur's audacious decision to cut Korea in two with an assault at Inchon by sea; or General Barry McCaffrey's famous "left hook" in the Persian Gulf completely bypassing most of the Iraqi Army.

In business, there are many situations where boldness can pay off big time. Billionaire Warren Buffet believes that the best time to buy stocks or companies is "when there is blood in the streets." When everyone else is selling, which was the case at the beginning of the great recession. Famous sports agent Leigh Steinberg became known for his opening negotiating proposals being so high, the other party saw them as outrageous.

Professionals know that boldness is called for when they have done extensive preparation, plotted a defensible strategy, and paid close attention to the details. As Leigh Steinberg says, "Others need to understand *why* you think you deserve what you are going to propose before you tell them *what* you are proposing."

If you want to ascend to the top of any profession, making the occasional bold move will accelerate your ability to get there. Pick your spots wisely but force yourself to make the move that others will see as outrageous when you know that your preparation has stacked the odds in your favor.

Amateurs Let Their Impatience Cause Them to Rush

Amateurs tend to be impatient. They have yet to develop the perspective that comes with experience. In the National Football League, rookies often talk about how fast the game seems to be compared to their experience in college. After a couple years in the league, these same players report that the game has slowed down. Of course, the pace is exactly the same, but they no longer have the nervousness that makes time seem like it is moving faster.

In business, amateurs are often "ready, fire, aim." They confuse activity with results. They rush from meeting to meeting and try and make too many decisions on the fly. When they attempt to force the pace out of nervousness or impatience, they continually find themselves in fire-fighting mode fixing problems of their own creation.

Professionals realize there are two kinds of time; strategic and tactical. Strategic time is weeks, months, or even years in advance of when something is to be completed. Rushing here is especially problematic because the most consequential decisions are the ones made up front. This is the *only* time when all your strategic options are available. Think about losing organizations in the world of professional sports. They fire their general manager and/or coach and rush to fill the vacancies not having fully understood why the team had failed or defining what kind of leaders they need going forward. They make knee-jerk decisions to hire people without thinking about long-term direction or data-based needs. Predictably, these organizations find themselves in exactly the same position a year or two later when the coach does not work out. The Cleveland

Browns, Jacksonville Jaguars, and San Francisco 49ers come readily to mind.

If you draw a vector with two lines and at the beginning these lines are only a degree apart, it does not seem like a big deal. But these lines carried out for miles cause the ending distance between them to be far off what was intended. So patience and diligence are called for when the decision is strategic to produce better long-term success. Your mind will not be cluttered by continual fire-fighting and you will be able to see the future more clearly. You will reserve the options that will allow you more flexibility in dealing with the unplanned events that always occur. Also, you will be better prepared to resist the temptation to bail out of your decision at the first sign of trouble.

Tactical time is shorter in nature. Your diligence in using strategic time effectively will be wasted if you do not execute the plan at the right time at a furious pace. Hesitation at the point of execution can be costly. Throw every available resource into execution, doing as the legendary UCLA Basketball Coach John Wooden advised, "Hurry but don't rush." Be focused and methodical on the job at hand. Save any second guessing you are tempted to do until later.

Amateurs Complain About the Generation Gap – Professionals Bridge It

"Is there really a generation gap?"[1] Of course there is! There has been one between each generational cohort in my lifetime. I am not a sociologist, but this is nothing new. As a person solidly in the middle of the Baby Boomer generation, I can assure you that my parents' generation was bewildered by how different we are from them. After all, they were the self-sacrificing lot that had saved the planet by winning World War II. We are the Me Generation – competitive, mercenary, passionate, individualistic, and distrusting of the very institutions they fought so hard to protect. (All true.)

As we Boomers grew older, we bemoaned Gen Xers as slackers. For the life of us we could not understand why they lacked the competitive fire that burns within us at work. (Mostly true.) Now the Millennials have arrived in their record numbers. Gen Xers see this group as needy, cynical, untrusting, and in some ways even more mercenary than the Boomers. (Probably true.)

So as I see it, we have two choices. Each generational cohort can sit around the campfire wringing their hands and blasting the others for not seeing the world the way they see it. Or we can direct our time and energy in a more productive pursuit of trying to figure out how to get the most out of working together.

Millennials now account for over half of the workers in the United States. A lot of them are still trying to figure out what they want out of their working life. Many hop from job to job trying to find themselves and praying that the next opportunity will be better than the last.

In the meantime, there is a storm brewing. Baby Boomers with their decades of tribal knowledge are fast fading into the sunset years. Millennials are not staying around long enough to absorb, let alone use the wisdom of their elders, and so the Boomers have stopped trying to teach and are taking this knowledge out the door with them as they retire. Basically, a reinforcing cycle. Why teach someone who will just leave, say the Boomers, which causes Millennials to leave because they aren't being taught.

I believe one solution is a re-dedication to mentoring. Creative Artists Agency in Los Angeles did a study in 2016 and found that 72 percent of Millennials would like to work for themselves. But 79 percent said that if they had to work for someone else, they want a boss that coaches and mentors them instead of merely directing them. Let's understand what most Millennials really want.

They desire:

- A steady stream of feedback. Not so much because they are needy, but because they want to know if they are good at what they do, if they are meeting expectations, and to find out what their professional weaknesses are.
- Tasks that are personally fulfilling.

- Work in an organization tied to a larger purpose.
- The opportunity to learn new skills.
- The chance to make new friends.
- Because they are in a hurry to become successful, they want meaningful work quickly with a minimum of needless bureaucracy.
- If we think about it, aren't these reasonable things to desire? Wouldn't Boomers and Gen Xers appreciate the same things?

In the organization's they join, they are looking for:

- One whose values match their own.
- An organization that will help them develop more skills.
- A clear career path that will allow them to reach their ultimate goals.
- Compensation and rewards that are customized to them.
- A place where their personal life blends with their work life in such a way that neither totally dominate.

Smart kids eh?

From a boss they want:

- Feedback on how they are doing.
- Flexibility in their work schedule.
- Being sponsored for internal and external development programs.
- Help in plotting a reasonable career path.
- Mentoring in the technical aspects of their work.
- Being seen as a partner with the boss rather than subservient.

So how does mentoring need to change?

- Mentors need to get past the idea that is not fair that they just give away knowledge that it took them decades to amass. It is vital to the ongoing success of the organization that mentoring be done. Organizations need to recognize this and give extra compensation for the mentoring older associates do.

- Mentors need to trust that in the right kind of culture, Millennials will choose to stay. That when they finally find a place that meets most of their needs, they won't jump ship for more money. And as each generation ages, the job-hopping naturally diminishes. So hopefully any knowledge mentors take the time to transfer will not be wasted.
- There should be mentoring by people outside the organization to augment what can be done internally.
- There are many areas where "online" mentoring might be worthwhile. Millennials are extremely comfortable doing things electronically.
- Group mentoring can occur selectively where one mentor can pass knowledge to many Millennials at the same time. This reduces cost and even if a few mentors leave, there is still a critical mass left with the information.
- No Mentor or Mentees should have anyone forced upon them.
- There should also be "reverse mentoring," where Millennials share what they know about social media and technology. Most people like to teach![2]

Tales from the Workplace

Doug Shane, Chairman of the Spaceship Company, has been leading the charge for many years to bring Sir Richard Branson's vision of commercializing space travel into fruition. Doug began his career as a test pilot. Back then, he developed the habit of visiting the work stations of everyone involved in building the aircraft he would someday fly. Even though he leans to the introverted side, Doug felt compelled to attempt to build relationships with everyone on the team. When I asked him why, he said only half-jokingly, "I thought that if they liked me they would take more care in what they were doing because they wouldn't want me to die."

As Doug moved up the ladder, he was mentored by the aviation pioneer Burt Rutan. In cutting-edge aerospace, much of the craft cannot be learned in school, so it is common for the "Grey Beards" to coach newer associates, though in a somewhat impersonal manner. Building a complex aircraft might be the ultimate team effort. The aircraft is built only as quickly and safely as the least skilled person on the team, so it is in everyone's interest to be helpful.

A few years later, Doug moved into the mentor role himself with his brand of coaching focusing on openness, honest dialog, courteous interactions, and professional respect. By the time he reached the executive level, Doug had seen enough of the time-honored tradition of the engineers being physically and relationally separated from the folks on the shop floor. He realized that an airplane could be built quicker, safer, and less expensively if those walls were torn down. So he created the "Desk Star" where the engineers who _designed_ things became embedded with those who _built_ things. Engineers' desks were literally moved onto the shop floor where true teamwork could evolve. The focus was now on manufacturability and not design overkill.

Doug sees one of his biggest challenges today being the changing composition of the workforce. As Millennials make up a much larger proportion of the workforce, how they are mentored becomes an issue. In Doug's view, the younger engineers are wickedly smart but they are used to more one-on-one styles of individualized mentoring and they want to be involved in everything right away. They often do not realize what they don't know and become frustrated with the older generation holding them back. Additionally, Millennial engineers seem to have trouble staying on schedule. Many have a tough time realizing there is a difference between "perfect" design and "good enough to be safe." Perfection may seem desirable in the bubble of the academic world, but in the real world of aerospace it is costly and incredibly time consuming. So individualized mentoring relationships become of paramount importance in bridging the gaps caused by the changing demographics of the workforce.

Professionals Continually Build their Social Capital

Harvard Professor Dr. Robert D. Putnam defines social capital as "the sum total of the implied or explicit promises that other people in your network have made to you." In effect, it is a bank account of goodwill that you can draw upon in future dealings with these people or others who may be influenced by these people. Numerous studies have shown that norms of reciprocity, mutual support, and trustworthiness are very strong in one's social network – in fact, many times stronger than with people we encounter outside our social circle.

Most people go through life in a transactional manner: I'll do this for you if you do this for me. This of course can be valuable if a fair trade can be established. The problem is that too often it becomes a sum zero game. We become richer in one area but find ourselves in a deficit in the area we just gave up. This type of social capital is more valuable if you already have an abundance of things to give away. It does not do us all that much good unless we are already "rich" to start with.[5]

Fortunately, there are strategies that will allow us to multiply our social capital. The most effective way is to give someone something without expecting anything specific back from them in return, confident that they or someone else will do something for you down the road.

Most people are afraid to do this as there is no *guarantee* that others will someday reciprocate. However, it is estimated that 93-95 percent of the time, people will repay the favor because most people hate to feel like they owe others. Sure we might get screwed 5-7 percent of the time, but here is the kicker. People who are helped in their time of need will not only repay you once, they will keep repaying you perhaps throughout the rest of your life. We have all heard stories of wealthy individuals leaving most of their fortune to someone not in the family who aided them when they were down and out. That is the multiplier effect.

A second way to build social capital is by facilitating introductions to others in your network who can benefit someone in need.

A couple years ago, I was the executive coach to a plant manager of an aerospace company. Through no fault of his own, he was fired because his plant did not meet truly impossible goals two years in a row (in this crazy company, *every* plant manager gets fired every few years for failing to do the impossible).

Now this fellow (we will call him Stan) did not understand the power of social capital and thus spent no time building a network outside his company. A couple months prior to his termination, Stan's wife had died leaving him to raise their children. One night he called me in desperation saying, "John you know my situation. The kids already lost their mother and I just can't uproot them from their friends too. I need to stay in Southern California but I have exhausted the few contacts in the industry that I have. Can you introduce me to people in your network that might need someone like me?"

I said sure Stan, no problem. The first person I thought of was Jerry. Jerry was a well-connected plant manager for a competing aerospace company in town. A two-minute phone call to Jerry went like this. "Jerry, how is the wife and family doing? Listen, I know you are busy, I need a favor. There is this guy that I have been coaching. He is great but works for that idiotic competitor of yours that fires plant managers every few years. He lost his job and for family reasons cannot afford to relocate outside this area. Could you meet with him and if you think he is talented, plug him into your network?" "Sure John, no problem," he replied.

Stan and Jerry hit it off and Jerry began introducing Stan in the local aerospace community. During this time, Jerry was promoted to Group CEO over several aerospace companies across the country. To backfill his old job as plant manager, he immediately installed Stan into the position. Of course, there is very little that Stan wouldn't do for me if I ever asked. But interestingly, even though technically I owe Jerry for his kindness, he feels he owes me. The way he sees it, I saved his company a $45,000.00 executive search fee by introducing him to someone who could competently fill his job immediately. All for a two-minute phone call!

The next time someone in your network asks you to connect them with someone, do it. When executive search firms contact you saying, "Do you know anyone who might be interested...." Give them a name. They will keep calling and one day you just might say, "You know, that sounds like something I might be a good fit for myself." I guarantee you that you will move to the top of that recruiters list.

A third way to build social capital is by letting others "save face" when they are backed into a corner. Most people continue to pile on grief to someone when they are wrong, make a mistake, or find themselves backed into a corner. This is futile because it puts the person on the defensive. He will fight harder to justify his position even if he knows he is wrong. He will try and blame shift responsibility for the mistake or you will have created an enemy for the future.

Most of us when we are wrong will admit it to ourselves. If we are treated kindly and tactfully, we might even admit it to others. But when someone tries to jam our mistakes down our throats, we get downright hostile. Every human being hates condemnation directed at them.

Tales from the Workplace

When I was 27 years old, I was hired as the head of staffing, training, and organization development for Caterpillar, Solar Turbines Division, in San Diego. The person I replaced had been terminated for poor performance. He was mid-forties in age and just happened to be the best friend of the head of compensation and benefits, Mike Verderber.

Now Mike and I had never met but he hated me sight unseen since I was this young kid chosen to replace his best friend. If you know anything about staffing, there needs to be a hand-in-glove relationship with compensation and benefits for jobs to be filled as there are frequent requests for exceptions to policy required to get top talent.

For my first two weeks, every single time I needed something from Mike, my requests were denied. Now I was also in charge of most HR policies outside of compensation and benefits. There was a woman named Julie who had come to the company six months earlier wanting to work in compensation. The company saw her as having management potential, so they put her into the management training program. Anyone in the program had to do eight three-month rotations in various parts of the company before they would be eligible for "permanent" assignment. Julie had only done two three-month rotations so she was not eligible to take a permanent position for another year and a half.

Mike petitioned me to allow Julie out of the management rotation program as he had an immediate opening in compensation. My boss knew there was an untenable problem between Mike and I. He did not want to command Mike to work with me as he knew that would only inflame the situation. But he sensed this was an opportunity to show Mike that I had some power too and that he needed me as much as I needed him.

My boss calls this big meeting of all the important players including Mike and I. He goes on a long spiel of how we in HR have got to be the role models to the rest of the company. If we let Julie out of the program early, we would be setting a precedent against our own policy, blah blah blah. He ended by saying, "But it is not my decision, IT IS JOHN'S."

My boss had put me in a position to stomp on Mike and deny his request, somehow equalizing the power between us. To my bosses complete shock (I later learned you should never surprise your boss in front of others), I said, "Boss, I understand your concern, but effective executives exist to make sensible exceptions to general rules. Now it was leaders in the company who put Julie in the management training program, not her. All she ever wanted was to work in compensation. Mike has a slot open now. In eighteen months when Julie is eligible for placement, he probably won't have an opening. I think I can defend this exception to the rest of the company, so I am going to allow Mike to have Julie."

My boss turned as red as a tomato, started stammering and stuttering, and abruptly called the meeting to a close. Within seconds, I was called into his office where for the next fifteen minutes, I received the worst verbal beating of my life. I was told in no uncertain terms that I was the dumbest person on the planet and other such niceties.

When I returned to my office, Mike was sitting there waiting. He closed my door and said, "Hey man, don't for a minute think that I don't know the beating you just took on my behalf. I have been there before. You know, I misjudged you. I guess I was upset that my best friend had been fired and I took it out on you. Today you showed me something. You did the right thing for me, for Julie, and for the company at great harm to yourself. Let's see if we can't work together."

Mike and I not only collaborated effectively together from that point on, he became my very best friend in the company. About six months later, my boss called me into his office to apologize. He said in effect, "I was the dumb one; I did not realize what you were trying to do regarding Mike. My way would have won a battle but lost a war. But next time, how about clueing me in beforehand."

Professionals Make Everyone Feel Important

Psychologists have long known that the need to feel significant in life is one of human beings' strongest needs. Most folks go to great lengths trying to be seen as special. This striving is what is behind people's desire to wear the latest fashions, own the coolest car or boat, brag about their children or grandchildren, or even join a movement such as ISIS. Think about when someone shows you a group photo that you are in. What do you look for first? Yourself of course.

The world is full of selfish attention seekers. If you become the type of person that can make others feel important rather than trying to outdo them yourself, you will possess an enormous advantage. You won't have a whole lot of competition out there.

Most of us have a tremendous level of pride. Because of this, we are more easily influenced if someone shows respect for the things we are proud of. Try and see issues and opportunities from the other person's point of view. Pay close attention to the hobbies they pursue. Then forward articles to them relating to their interests. By connecting via their interests, you are confirming that what they do for fun is important and by extension that they are important.

My friend Bernie Clayton knows that I never miss a single play of a Pittsburgh Steelers game. My father and I went to every home game they played from the time I was five years old until I graduated from high school. They were my first employer after college. So I have fond memories every time I see the Steelers play. Bernie sends me a text during every game commenting on how he sees the team performing. He keeps articles from *Sports Illustrated* that mention the Steelers and forwards interesting commentary to me about the team that he hears from other sources. The interesting thing is Bernie never had any connection with the Steelers until he met me. Now he pays almost as much attention to them as I do, and that makes me feel that I am important to him.

A critical thing in making people feel important is remembering their names. Calling a person by name creates an instant feeling of goodwill, while forgetting their name feels like a kick in the gut to them. Half the time when I am talking to people for the first time, they can't even remember my name by the time the conversation was over.[6]

Most of us fail to remember names because we were not really concentrating on it when we first heard it. People who are great at remembering names like my friend Hedley Lawson, says that it helps if you repeat their name several times during the conversation. This will imprint the name into your memory.

LinkedIn lets you know when people in your network have a birthday coming up or when they received promotion or a new job. Get in the habit of taking a few minutes each day to send a little note of congratulations.

Ask peoples advice on things in which you know they have an interest. Everyone loves to talk about subjects that they feel like they have some knowledge of. This shows that you thought they were important enough to ask. Every single person that I asked to tell me a story for this book said they felt honored that I would even ask. And those who you have read about are people who are far more successful than I.

For many years, I was on the executive campaign committee of the San Diego United Way. Every year people who had contributed the prior year and did not contribute in the current year, were asked why they no longer gave to the campaign. The number one answer by far was that they were not thanked for their donation the year before. People may do things for their own selfish reasons, but they sure want to be appreciated for what they do. We all have a need to feel important!

CONCLUSION

"There are two things to aim at in life:
First, to get what you want; and after that to enjoy it."

Logan Pearsall Smith

IN READING THIS book, you and I have started on a journey together. How much further down the road you go is up to you. Building successful relationships is most likely important to you. You may already be great at relating to others and want to continue to improve. Or you may have been frustrated with your ability to get what you want out of one or more relationships. Hopefully the stories told by successful people have enlightened and inspired you. Putting the insights and ideas presented in the "A Quick Guide to Improving" segments of each chapter will equip you with what you need to improve the quality of the relationships in your life at home and as a leader at work.

I hope you agree that interpersonal effectiveness begins with you accepting responsibility for doing the things necessary to become more easy to relate to – that it is not about learning to fix, change, manipulate, or control someone else. Now that you have finished reading what I have written, you can be satisfied that you have become a bit wiser and continue life as you lived it before. Or you can dedicate yourself to taking your leadership to the next level through diligent application of those nuggets in the book that resonated most with you.

You should not expect that you will experience an overnight transformation in your relationships. Change does not work that way. We know that crash diets seldom sustain weight loss. It would be unrealistic to be able to run 26.2 miles the first time you put on running shoes or lift your maximum weight at the gym the first time you go. Behavioral change is much the same. Step-by-step increments ultimately leading to your goals will give you the best chance at sustaining whatever changes you decide to make.

You have behaved your way into your current state with others and you will have to behave differently to change the trajectory of your life. Some things presented here will be "low hanging fruit," very easy for you to pick to adopt immediately. Others will take some time and more concentrated effort. The ultimate challenge is to make the elements that will allow you to have more satisfying and productive relationships habitual – meaning the style adjustments you make have been repeated often enough that you do them without much effort or thought.

The nice thing about self-improvement is that there is a hidden benefit called the multiplier effect. Small changes lead to improvements that will cause even more improvements. Growth inevitably leads to more growth. The first step is to start today making an effort to put into practice the most important thing you have learned from reading this book. Then go on to the next most important thing and before long, you will have arrived at a new and better destination relationship wise.

When you Win with Style, there are no losers.

END NOTES

Introduction

1. ESPN Sports Center, 12-30-2015
2. USA Today, Daniel Uthman, 1-7-2016

Chapter 2

1. Wall Street Journal, 2-24-2014

Chapter 3

1. *Emotional Intelligence*, Daniel Goleman, New York: Bantam Books, 1995
2. Handbook of Mental Control, V5 Englewood Cliffs, NJ: Prentice Hall, 1993
3. *Emotional Intelligence*, Ibid
4. Reuters, October 25, 2014
5. CBS/Associated Press, April 12, 2007
6. Jon Boon, July 25, 2015
7. Beau HD, Mashable.com, October 15, 2016
8. *The Five Languages of Apology*, Gary Chapman and Jennifer Thomas, 2006 Northfield Publishing
9. Fleet Street Fox, January 18, 2013
10. Wikipedia

11. Tori Rodriguez, January 1, 2016. *What You Wear Can Influence Your Thinking and Negotiating Skills, Even Hormone Levels and Heart Rate.* Scientific American.
12. *The New Art of Managing People*, Phil Hunsaker and Tony Alessandra, Free Press, 2008
13. *The New Art of Managing People*, Ibid
14. Kenneth W. Thomas, *Conflict & Conflict Management*, 1977
15. Handbook of Industrial and Organizational Psychology. Rand McNally 1976

Chapter 4

1. Hamilton Jordan, *Crisis* (New York: Putnam 1982)
2. Mark Burnett, *Jump In* (New York: Random House 2005)
3. Jeffrey Pfeffer, *Power in Organizations* (Marsh Field, MA, Pitman Publishing, 1981) P101
4. USA Today, *Ford Benefits from CEO; Turn to Road Less Traveled*, Sharon Silke Carty, December 10, 2008 p.2
5. James MacGregor Burns, *Leadership* (New York: Harper & Row, 1978)
6. DreamWorks Home Entertainment, *The Last Castle*, 2001

Chapter 5

1. CNBC, 9-23-2015
2. Huffington Post, 10-9, 2015
3. Bloomberg Businessweek, 11-16-2016 Perry Williams, David Stringer, Jesse Riseborough
4. USA Today, 11-25-2013
5. Wikipedia
6. CNN, 5-23-2014
7. ABC News, 9-8-2016
8. Freedom Outpost, 3-11-2016, Tim Brown
9. Wikipedia
10. CNN 2-27-2015, Jeremy Diamond

11. Tolero Solutions
12. Bill George, *Authentic Leadership; Rediscovering the Secrets to Creating Lasting Value* (San Francisco: Jossey-Bass, 2003)
13. Interview with Fred Howard, 12-27-2016
14. Interview with Mike Burns, 11-11-2008
15. Carly Fiorina, *Tough Choices,* Portfolio, 2006
16. Fuel Fix, Jordan Blum, 12-3-2015
17. Colette Symanowitz: *Why Do CEO's Get Fired*, 10-10-2013
18. Benjamin Zander, *The Art of Possibility: Transforming Professional and Personal Life*, Penguin, 2002
19. Cari Ressler and Jody Thompson, *Why Work Sucks: And How to Fix That* (New York: Penguin Group, 2008)
20. John Huntsman, *Winners Never Cheat: Even in Difficult Times*, Wharton School Publishing, 2008
21. Quote often attributed to both Steven R. Covey and Dr. Phil McGraw
22. Interview with Chris Carroll, 12-27-2016
23. William D. Hitt, *Ethics and Leadership* (Columbus, Ohio Battelle Press, 1990) p. 99

Chapter 6

1. Jim Collins, *Good to Great: Why Some Companies Make the Leap and Others Don't.* (New York: Harper Collins, 2001) p.21
2. Interview with Launie Fleming, 12-26-2016
3. Roger Connors and Tom Smith, *Journey to the Emerald City* (Paramus, NJ Prentice Hall Press, 1999) p. 32
4. Interview with Chris Carroll, 12-27-2016
5. Consulting work with US Navy Seal Teams, Coronado, CA 1988

Chapter 7

1. *Stress Processing Report*, Human Synergistics, 1988
2. Robert Greene, *The 48 Laws of Power*. New York: Penguin Group, 2000

3. Barry Schwartz, *The Paradox of Choice*. New York: Harper Perennial, 2004

4. Jeanne C. Meister and Karie Willyerd, *Mentoring Millennials*: Harvard Business Review, October 2016

5. Robert D. Putnam: *Bowling Alone: The Collapse and Revival of American Community*, Touchstone, New York, 2000

6. Dale Carnegie: *How to Win Friends and Influence People*. Fingerpaint, New Delhi, 2016

ABOUT EFFECTIVENESS DIMENSIONS INTERNATIONAL

FOR OVER 31 years, Effectiveness Dimensions International has been in the business of helping leaders and organizations increase their effectiveness. More than 27,000 managers from over 1,700 organizations have attended the Dr. John W. Hanes Leadership Academy Seminar.

Some examples of our services include:

- Public and In-House sessions of the Leadership Academy Seminar
- Three-hour Executive Candidate Assessment Interviews
- One-on-one Executive Coaching
- Organization Effectiveness Analysis
- Team Effectiveness Analysis
- 360 Degree Assessment
- Psychometric Profiles
- Training Simulations

To order copies of the Interpersonal Preferences Profile, or any of our other assessment instruments, go to: www.EffectivenessDimensions.com

To register to attend a public session of the Dr. John W. Hanes Leadership Academy Seminar, go to: www.TeamTopGun.com

To order additional copies of *Winning with Style*, go to: www.WinningWithStyle.net

To order copies of Dr. John W. Hanes previous book, *Change Focused Leadership*, go to: www.Amazon.com

Headquarters
Effectiveness Dimensions International
P.O. Box 839
Lake Arrowhead, CA 92352
www.EffectivenessDimensions.com
+1-909-336-3675

ABOUT DR. JOHN W. HANES

DR. JOHN HANES is an international authority on individual and organizational effectiveness. His extraordinary background has placed him in a unique position to help leaders increase their effectiveness; here are a few highlights from Dr. Hanes experiences:

- Doctorate in Leadership Effectiveness – University of San Diego
- Master's and Bachelor's degrees in Business – Case Western and University of Cincinnati
- Visiting Scholar at the Battelle Memorial Institute, 1988-1990
- Visiting Scholar at the Center for Creative Leadership, 1986-1988
- Adjunct faculty – San Diego State University, 1984-1986
- President – Effectiveness Dimensions, 1985-Present
- Author – *Change Focused Leadership* (2009)
- Psychological Instrumentation Expert – Author of 11 Instruments and 7 Simulations
- Consultant to over 1,700 organizations including Fortune 500 companies, federal, state, local government agencies, non-profit and small privately held business entities
- Consultant to 1997 "Oscar" winner
- Consultant to 6 NFL "All Pro" players, 1990-1995
- Honored by American Society for Training and Development for International Excellence, 1986

- Executive Cabinet – United Way, 1985-1989, 2000-2002
- Former Executive at Key Bank and Caterpillar, 1977-1985
- Former "Scout" Pittsburgh Steelers, 1976-1977 season
- Personally trained over 27,000 managers 1985 to present

Dr. John W. Hanes is president of Effectiveness Dimensions International, a leadership consulting firm based in southern California. For additional information, visit www.WinningWithStyle.net or www.TeamTopGun.com.

CPSIA information can be obtained
at www.ICGtesting.com
Printed in the USA
LVOW11*0251220217
524980LV00002B/2/P